GREG L. HAWKINS AND CALLY PARKINSON

FOREWORD BY **JOHN ORTBERG**

AFTE

WHAT'S NEXT
FOR YOU?

JOHN ORTBERG

Pastor
Menlo Park Presbyterian Church

FOREWORD

It's hard to imagine something more difficult to gauge or measure than spiritual growth. There is a mystery to it. It is intangible. It is like the wind, which blows wherever it pleases; you hear its sound, but you cannot tell where it comes from or where it is going.

Yet there is only one thing I can think of more foolish than trying to gauge spiritual growth. And that is: not trying to gauge it. For that which matters to us is that which we try to keep track of.

People in the church have attempted to measure spiritual growth ever since the winds blew on the day of Pentecost and somebody counted baptisms (three thousand). In our day, writers like Dallas Willard and Ron Sider have cited study after study demonstrating how church-attending, Bible-believing Christians do not behave any differently than their secular counterparts. This is not just a problem; it is a tragedy and a scandal. Assessing when and how spiritual transformation happens may be hard. But we have to try.

I am part of a church that participated in one of the first REVEAL surveys. And we learned more from this one survey about what's working and what's not than from anything else we've ever tried.

I was also in the auditorium at Willow Creek when an overview of the initial REVEAL results was presented at the Leadership Summit in 2007. You could hear thousands of church leaders responding to the single finding that was to me the most important and unsettling: that as spiritual life progresses, increased involvement in church activities ceases to predict spiritual growth. I have rarely heard information that was such a surprise when it was announced, yet made intuitive sense to all the church leaders as soon as it sunk in. The emperor's clothes have left the building.

But there are deeper and richer veins of information to be mined. What are the spiritual attitudes and beliefs that actually catalyze movement from one stage to another? What are the practices that people find most helpful as they travel toward God? How do churches find "best practices" when it comes not just to putting on services or raising funds, but in helping Christ to be formed in people?

So here is round two, *Follow Me*. Read it through. Learn from it. Use it to inform your ministry. Pick it apart. Argue with it. Critique it. Try to find better ways to measure spiritual growth. Try to figure out why/how/if it can be measured at all.

REVEAL is prompting churches and church leaders to roll up their sleeves and get serious about facing up to how we are *actually doing* at being part of the transformation of human lives.

Read it and change.

John Ortberg

John Ortberg

PREVIEW

When we say "Follow me" to those we lead, we want to be absolutely sure we know where we're going and how we plan to get there. However, when it comes to spiritual growth, it's not always clear how best to do that. What if we could know with confidence that the steps we're asking people to take will actually move them closer to Christ? Would it change the way you lead?

How does spiritual growth happen? How do we help people move toward a more intimate and committed relationship to Christ? We examine four powerful categories of spiritual catalysts that inspire growth across the spiritual continuum.

Spiritual growth needs are dramatically different for early believers compared to committed Christ-followers. What does and does not inspire growth at different stages of spiritual development? We dive deep into the research to find out.

The spiritual journey is not without its frustrations. Many churchgoers say they are derailed from their relationship with God or the church. How does this happen? What are the barriers that get in the way of spiritual growth? And what can we do about them?

WHAT'S NEXT FOR YOU?

"Anyone who wants to be my disciple must follow me, because my servants must be where I am." (*John 12:26a NLT*)

The divine refrain heard by every would-be believer
is captured in two simple words: *follow me.*

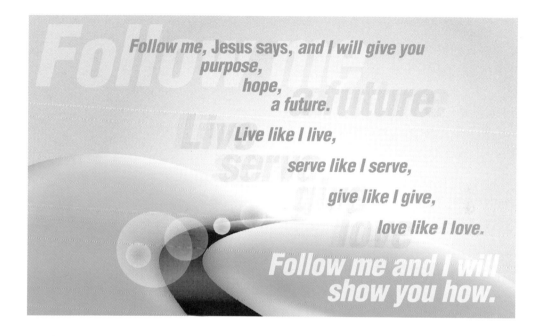

Follow me, Jesus says, and I will give you
purpose,
hope,
a future.
Live like I live,
serve like I serve,
give like I give,
love like I love.
Follow me and I will
show you how.

It is the goal of every church leader:
    To guide followers in the footsteps of Jesus.
    To point them toward growth and transformation,
        healing and wholeness,
            intimacy with God and others.
    To help them move from where they are to where they want to be.

But how does this happen?
Which things *truly* help to move people toward Christ . . .
And which things don't?

Can spiritual growth be predicted?
    Catalyzed?
        Measured?

What causes a person to shift from kicking the tires of Christianity to surrendering wholeheartedly to God?

If we knew the answers, would it change the way we do church?

A year ago, REVEAL asked the question: "Where are you?"

Eighty thousand people in 200 congregations responded.

Thousands of people responded:
> *I am . . .*
>> *Exploring Christ*
>> *Growing in Christ*
>> *Close to Christ*
>> *Christ-Centered.*

And these answers prompted more questions.

"Based on where you are," we wanted to know,
"Is this where you want to be?
If not, then where is God calling you?
What's next for you?
How can we help?"

Eighty thousand people in 200 congregations responded.

Their gut-level insights—what they really want from the church, the barriers they face, what draws them closer to Christ—may surprise you.

The good news?
They want to follow Christ.

The challenge?
We have to change the way we lead.

Pull up a chair as the conversation continues . . .
about the truth of spiritual growth,
and about the next steps that we can take together.

GREG L. HAWKINS

1

FOLLOW THE LEADER

WHAT PEOPLE REALLY WANT FROM THE CHURCH AND ITS LEADERS

confidence

WHEN WE SAY "FOLLOW ME" to those we lead, we want to be absolutely sure we know where we're going and how we plan to get there. However, when it comes to spiritual growth, it's not always clear how best to do that. What if we could know with confidence that the steps we're asking people to take will actually move them closer to Christ? Would it change the way you lead?

1

FOLLOW
THE LEADER

I remember saying "yes" to following Jesus. Actually, for me, it was a two-part decision. The first yes was to receive his forgiveness for my sins; the second yes came a few years later when I gave him full authority over my life. My life was his to use, however he wanted to use it. And from that second yes almost thirty years ago, I have continued to try, with his help, to say yes to him every single day. Saying yes to Jesus and surrendering to his leadership have profoundly changed me.

Jesus' call to "follow me" has no doubt profoundly impacted you, as well. At some point in time, you received Christ's invitation, you said yes, and you began to walk a new path with him. In fact, you're likely in ministry today because you were so profoundly impacted that you decided to make following Jesus —and helping others to do the same—the focus of your life's work.

As ministry leaders, we are impassioned—often fanatically so— about helping people establish intimacy with Jesus Christ. We are hungry to see men and women freed up from the things that weigh them down and to see spiritual transformation take place. But out of the hundred things we *could* have them do, which ones will really accomplish that goal?

Whether we serve vocationally or as volunteers, it's rarely a lack of motivation that trips us up in our quest to catalyze spiritual growth in those we lead; it's knowing how to actually *get it done*. Every week,

How do we know if the path we've chosen will really make a difference in people's lives?

The people in your church really want to grow closer to Christ.

we stand in front of teams or congregations and say, "Follow me!" It's what leaders do—we *lead*. But how do we know if the path we've chosen will really make a difference in people's lives? How do we know if our churches are getting it right?

In an effort to find out, we recently conducted new research in which we heard from 80,000 people in more than 200 churches. We learned all kinds of things, but one thing in particular really jumped out at me. When we asked, "What's the most important thing you want from your church?" one of the top answers was, "Challenge me to grow and take the next step in my spiritual life."

Did you catch that?

They didn't say that they come to our churches to hear great teaching or meet new friends. They want to be challenged. They want to grow. They want to take the next steps and see progress.

The people in your church really want to grow closer to Christ. And they're looking to you—their leader—wondering if you can help them. Imagine that! They stand in front of you, desperately wanting you to say, "Follow me." And with their next breath, they ask the simple question, "Can you really help me change?"

LEADING CHANGE

Throughout my career, I've learned a lot about change. And over and over again, whether it was leading people in my church or as a management consultant helping a business through a time of change, I first needed to discover the answer to two simple questions: *Where are they now?* and *Where do they want to be?* The difference between where they are and where they want to be creates a gap—a vision gap.

Peter Senge, director of the Center for Organizational Learning at MIT's Sloan School of Management, talks about this gap being the distance between reality and vision. While these are different terms, they

Follow me. We know that Jesus said these words. In fact, he said them many times, creating a theme that runs throughout his public ministry on earth.

At the beginning of his ministry, as he walked along the Sea of Galilee, Jesus uttered these words to the first two disciples he called, the fishermen brothers, Peter and Andrew: "'Come, follow me, and I will show you how to fish for people!' And they left their nets at once and followed him" (*Matthew 4:19–20 NLT*). Amazingly, at the very beginning of his ministry on earth, Jesus established himself as a leader by calling these individuals to follow him. Their responsibility was to accept the invitation, and if they did, he promised to show them how to fish for people.

Later, when some of the Jewish people challenged whether or not Jesus was the Messiah promised by their prophets, he answered, "My sheep listen to my voice; I know them, and they follow me. I give them eternal life, and they shall never perish; no one can snatch them out of my hand" (*John 10:27–28*). Again, Jesus seemed to be talking about the responsibility that comes with following him, reminding us that his followers don't simply claim their faith in him, they also walk with him in obedience based on their love for him.

Even near the end of his earthly ministry, after his entry into Jerusalem, Jesus said, "Whoever serves me must follow me; and where I am, my servant also will be. My Father will honor the one who serves me" (*John 12:26*).

After Jesus explained to his disciples that he would suffer, be rejected and be crucified as Savior and Messiah, he invited the disciples to go down the same difficult path: "If any of you wants to be my follower, you must turn from your selfish ways, take up your cross daily, and follow me. If you try to hang on to your life, you will lose it. But if you give up your life for my sake, you will save it" (*Luke 9:23–24 NLT*).

This theme continued even after the resurrection, when Jesus asked Peter three times to declare his love for him. Peter answered, "Lord, you know all things; you know that I love you" (*John 21:17*). Jesus seemed to want action more than Peter's words, so he commanded, "Feed my sheep . . . Follow me!" (*John 21:17, 19*). ✦

fit nicely with the questions of where we are now (reality) and where we want to be (vision). In his book *The Fifth Discipline*, Senge notes that the gap itself provides the energy we need to move from where we are now to where we want to be. He calls this gap "creative tension." I like the illustration Senge uses to describe the creative tension that comes along with change.

"Imagine a rubber band, stretched between your vision and current reality. When stretched, the rubber band creates tension, representing the tension between vision and current reality. What does the tension seek? Resolution or release. There are only two possible ways for the tension to resolve itself: pull reality toward the vision or pull the vision toward reality. Which occurs will depend on whether we hold steady to the vision."[1]

The Creative Tension Gap

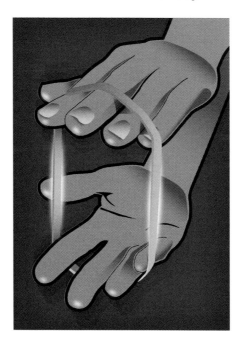

In other words, when you feel the tension in the gap between where you are and where you want to be, you realize that the tension needs to be released. You can either lower your aspirations about where you want to be, or you can create plans and strategies that move you closer from where you are to where you want to be.

Here's a practical example of this principle. Like most Americans, I wrestle with maintaining my weight. Last year I went to the doctor for my annual physical. On the way to the exam room, the nurse asked me

---

[1] Peter M. Senge, *The Fifth Discipline: The Art and Practice of the Learning Organization* (New York: Doubleday, 2006), 140.

to step on the scale; it registered my weight as 205 pounds. By the way, why do doctor's office scales always add at least five pounds to what you weigh? Anyway, when it comes to my weight, that's the answer to the first question: *Where am I now?* I weigh 205 pounds.

At the end of my exam, the doctor told me that for my height—as well as for the sake of my heart and my cholesterol levels—I should weigh 185 pounds. That's the answer to the second question: *Where do I want to be?* I should weigh 185 pounds.

The *gap* is simply the difference between the two answers. When it comes to my weight, the gap is twenty pounds.

The size of the gap is important.

Interestingly, when it comes to change, the size of the gap is important. If the gap is too small, I might not have much motivation or energy to work for making the change. If the gap is too large, I might be overwhelmed and lose all hope of ever making a change. Back to my weight, if I only had to lose five pounds, I might not give it much attention. On the other hand, if I had to lose seventy-five pounds, I might give up before I ever tried.

Of course, no matter how big or small the gap is, just knowing the gap isn't enough. For change to occur, we need to come up with a workable plan to close the gap. And the plan needs to include specific steps that also reflect all the other realities that have to be dealt with. Again, back to my weight, if I want to close the gap and lose twenty pounds, I know it's unrealistic to think I can carve out an hour every day to exercise. With a family and a busy job and other commitments, that plan isn't workable. So I not only need specific steps, I need specific steps that account for the other realities in my life. Instead of exercising an hour every day, my plan to lose twenty pounds might include exercising three times a week for thirty minutes, drinking more water, snacking on fresh fruit instead of candy bars and eating more lean protein and vegetables at mealtimes.

For change to occur, we need to come up with a workable plan to close the gap.

DISCERNING THE GAPS IN SPIRITUAL GROWTH

As leaders, we must establish the right amount of tension in order to catalyze change.

What does this gap mean for us as church leaders? I think it means that if the people in our congregations are saying, "Challenge me to grow and take the next step in my spiritual life," then we need to start by discerning the gaps in their spiritual growth. Remember, the gap is simply the distance between the current situation (*Where are we now?*), and our vision for the future (*Where do we want to be?*).

Keep in mind that if the vision doesn't boldly take us beyond our current reality, it won't produce much tension. But if the vision seems so outrageously different than our current reality, the rubber band will snap and no tension will remain because people will lose hope. As leaders, we must establish the right amount of tension in order to catalyze change.

Once we discern the gaps, we can then offer plans with specific steps to help people close the gaps in their spiritual growth. Of course, we don't want to create a plan with a hundred steps! We provide just the first three or four steps in order to create some movement toward closing the gap. These steps probably won't close the gap entirely, but as people accomplish these first few steps, then we provide the next three or four steps to take.

RIGHT-SIZING THE SPIRITUAL GAP

Now, what if I really got serious about losing weight and getting in shape? I mean, let's say that I liked this new healthy feeling so much that I decided to work with a personal trainer to take the next steps. If that trainer is worth the hourly fee, I'd soon understand the gap in my physical life and create a workable plan for closing it.

In the church, leaders need to take on a similar role. We need to become something like spiritual trainers or coaches who help people process the two questions that can help them define their gaps: *Where am I now?* and *Where do I want to be?* And then we can help them consider the question, *What's next for me?* Let's take a closer look at each of these questions.

Where Am I Now?

Or to use Peter Senge's term, what's my current "reality"? To answer this question in terms of growing spiritually, you help people wrestle with some digging-deeper questions like: Is my spiritual life as shallow as I think it is? How "good" is good enough? How does God really see me?

Where Do I Want to Be?

Again, to use Senge's term, what's my "vision" of where God wants me to be? To answer this question in terms of growing spiritually, you help individuals wrestle with meaningful questions like: What is the goal when it comes to spiritual growth? What does a follower of Jesus look like? How do I know if I've arrived spiritually? How does my spiritual life connect to the rest of my life?

What's Next for Me?

At this point, we need to keep in mind what we've discovered about the gap. If the gap seems too insignificant, people won't think the changes are worth the effort. And if the gap seems too enormous, people will find the challenge too overwhelming and give up before they try. If the vision we cast involves "forty-seven steps to becoming more like Jesus," it might seem like an impossible target no matter how well we present those steps. The rubber band snaps, the creative tension disappears and people simply lose all hope.

But when the gap is right-sized, healthy tension is held and movement is made toward getting it closed. Of course, closing the gap spiritually isn't like losing twenty pounds. As much as we might want to, we can't create a simple plan to become more like Christ in the next sixty days.

What is the goal when it comes to spiritual growth?

We need to help people remember that while we all must take steps to grow closer to Christ, he's the one who accomplishes the changes. Our task is to align ourselves with God's will and purposes and allow the Holy Spirit to do the work.

Our Challenge

Further, our challenge as spiritual coaches is to personalize these steps for the people in our congregations—designing the first or next steps someone needs to take, keeping in mind that not everyone needs to take the same next steps. It takes a lot of discernment to help someone figure out where to go next.

It takes a lot of discernment to help someone figure out where to go next.

Because this personalizing can be so difficult, our churches often default to creating a lot of ministries, and we tell people to do all of them! While most or all of these programs and ministries might be sound and biblically based, we really haven't succeeded in helping people determine the gaps they need to close as individuals. Yet, remember what the latest research is telling us? People in our churches are saying, "Challenge me to grow and take the next step in my spiritual life." And they expect this challenge to come from you! What do you do?

RESOLVING THE TENSION

In January 2007, we surveyed seven congregations, including Willow Creek. We heard from 5,000 congregants. Our goal was to understand the practical ways in which people grow spiritually. As a result of that research, we identified a way to probe people's attitudes, motivations and behaviors, and how to place them in one of four spiritual segments based on how important or central Christ is in their lives (chart 1-2).

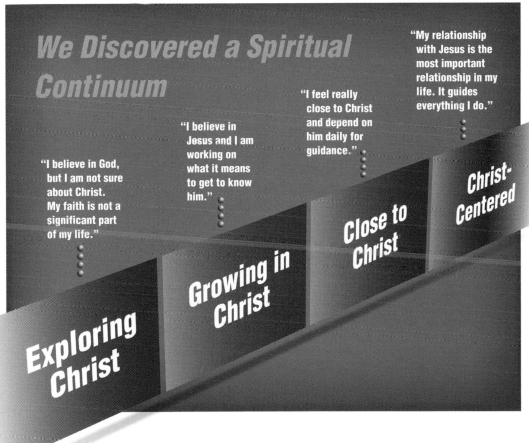

Chart 1-2: This framework emerged in our original research as the most powerful predictive description of how people grow spiritually.

We published our findings in *Reveal*. Briefly, the four segments are as follows:

Exploring Christ

The people in this group have a basic belief in God, but they're unsure about Christ and his role in their lives.

We want to understand how real people actually go about closing the spiritual gaps in their lives.

Growing in Christ

The people in this group have a personal relationship with Christ. They've made a commitment to trust him with their salvation and for their eternity, but they are just beginning to learn what it means to be in a relationship with him.

Close to Christ

The people in this group depend on Christ daily for their lives. They see Christ as someone who assists them in life. On a daily basis, they turn to him for help and guidance for issues they face.

Christ-Centered

The people in this group would identify their relationship with Christ as the most important relationship in their entire lives. They see their lives as fully surrendered to Jesus and his agenda, subordinating everything to his will and his desires.

Identifying these segments gave pastors and church leaders a good framework to figure out where people are. But just knowing where they are is not enough. Our ultimate goal is to understand how people actually grow to become more like Jesus. Or, using the gap analogy, we want to understand how real people actually go about closing the spiritual gaps in their lives.

So in November and December 2007 we surveyed 200 additional congregations. Large churches, small churches. Denominational, independent. North, East, South, West. We heard from over 80,000 congregants who answered questions from our new, modified survey tool. And the good news is that we've uncovered a deeper understanding of how we can really help people move from one segment to the next.

WHAT OUR SOULS FLOW TOWARD

I recently came across a poem by Mary Oliver titled "Gravel." In it she describes how it is the nature of stones to be "satisfied." In contrast, she writes, water longs to be "somewhere else."

How true. Stones just sit there; they don't move. They don't even desire movement. By nature, they're just static. However, water is very different. It always seeks to move. It can't keep still and it changes direction all the time.

We humans are like water.
In fact, around 60 percent of our body is made up of water. And like water, we constantly search for something else—some other place that our souls flow toward. Whether we know it or not, what we want to flow toward is God. We want deep intimacy—to be reconnected to God as we were in the very beginning, as we were intended to be.

Whether we know it or not, what we want to flow toward is God.

People want to follow you because they believe that you'll help them grow closer to Christ.

As pastors and leaders, our task isn't to just help people in some random pursuit of a better life. Rather, it is to really guide people toward a life lived in deep communion with God through Jesus Christ—a life filled with purpose and meaning, a life not just about oneself, a life surrendered to Christ and committed to serving others.

Whether or not you say the words "Follow me," that's the invitation you extend as a leader in your church or area of ministry. And people want to follow you because they believe that you'll help them grow closer to Christ. They believe you'll help them meet the challenge of taking the next steps in their spiritual lives. And the great news is that you can! You can help people understand both where they are and where they want to be—where God wants them to be. You can provide the specific next steps to coach the people in your church to help them move forward. That's what the rest of this book is all about. Our hope is that you will discover insights to lead yourself and your congregation toward deeper intimacy with Christ.

CALLY PARKINSON

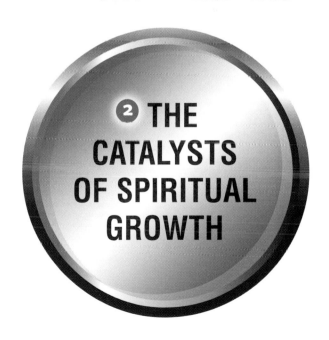

2 THE
CATALYSTS
OF SPIRITUAL
GROWTH

CORE BELIEFS AND ACTIVITIES THAT INSPIRE SPIRITUAL GROWTH

catalysts

HOW DOES SPIRITUAL GROWTH HAPPEN? How do we help people move toward a more intimate and committed relationship to Christ? We examine four powerful categories of spiritual catalysts that inspire growth across the spiritual continuum.

2

THE CATALYSTS
OF SPIRITUAL GROWTH

Think about the last airplane trip you took. If you were in a window seat, you probably watched a city landscape come into focus as the plane made its descent. You saw roads and buildings changing from a distant mix of shapes and lights to a set of distinct landmarks and structures. The closer the plane came to landing, the more you were able to see the details below— the movement of vehicles and people going about their daily lives.

We've had a similar experience—moving from a distant to a more detailed view—over the course of our research into what drives spiritual growth. Our first discoveries painted a picture of the spiritual landscape in broad strokes. We identified a spiritual continuum of four segments defined by attitudes, motivations and behaviors that characterized different stages of spiritual growth (chart 2-1, page 26).

We identified a spiritual continuum of four segments defined by attitudes, motivations and behaviors.

We discussed in broad terms the significant role the church plays in the earlier stages of spiritual growth and the powerful influence of personal spiritual practices across all segments on the continuum.

This initial picture was clear, but also somewhat limited. Our early findings, published in *Reveal* in 2007, were based on approximately 5,000 surveys from just seven churches. Although we chose the churches intentionally—for diversity of size, geography and format—the scope of our findings was still limited to a narrow slice of churches.

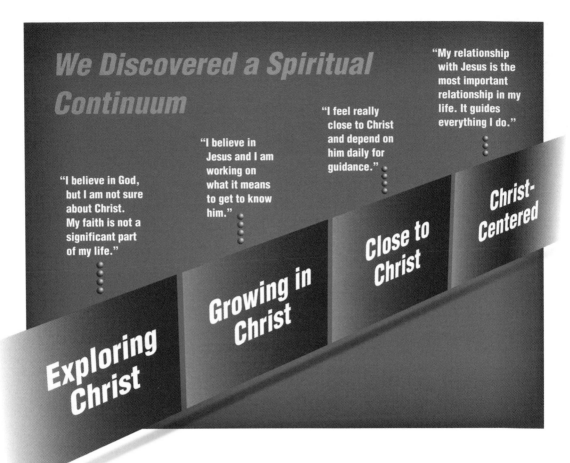

We Discovered a Spiritual Continuum

"I believe in God, but I am not sure about Christ. My faith is not a significant part of my life."

"I believe in Jesus and I am working on what it means to get to know him."

"I feel really close to Christ and depend on him daily for guidance."

"My relationship with Jesus is the most important relationship in my life. It guides everything I do."

Exploring Christ

Growing in Christ

Close to Christ

Christ-Centered

Chart 2-1: This framework emerged in our original research as the most powerful predictive description of how people grow spiritually. We discovered that spiritual attitudes and behaviors increase significantly in frequency and intensity as people move across the continuum.

Today those limitations are a distant memory. Our latest findings are based on a database of nearly 80,000 surveys from congregants in over 200 churches. These churches represent a wide range of sizes, geographies, styles, ethnicities and denominations (see appendix 3, "Who Are the 200 Churches in the Survey?" on page 151). The depth and breadth of this expanded database gives us a much closer view of the dynamics of spiritual development as well as insights about what drives—and derails—spiritual growth.

The focus of this book is spiritual movement: specifically, what moves a person from one stage of spiritual growth to the next. Just like the window view from a descending plane, we're now able to look beyond the big picture findings and focus more closely on what goes on in the spaces between the four segments on the spiritual continuum. What we see is that most people are not standing still. While there are some who are stalled, unable to make progress in their spiritual journey, most are moving—in many cases, rapidly—toward a more intimate relationship with Christ.

The focus of this book is spiritual movement: specifically, what moves a person from one stage of spiritual growth to the next.

FOUR CATEGORIES
OF SPIRITUAL CATALYSTS

In the REVEAL survey, we measured over fifty factors to assess their impact on spiritual growth. These factors ranged from personal activities, like daily prayer; to organized church activities, like weekend worship services; to the core beliefs central to the Christian faith, like belief in the Trinity.[1] We've collected these fifty factors into the following four categories of spiritual catalysts.

Catalyst 1

Spiritual beliefs and attitudes: Core Christian beliefs, such as belief in salvation by grace or the authority of the Bible.

Catalyst 2

Organized church activities: The most common activities organized by the church, such as weekend worship services, small groups, adult education classes on spiritual topics or serving in a church ministry.

[1] "The Trinity," is our shorthand for referring to people's agreement with this statement: "I believe the God of the Bible is the one true God—Father, Son and Holy Spirit."

Catalyst 3

Personal spiritual practices: Personal disciplines that develop a person's faith, such as prayer, reflection on Scripture or solitude.

Catalyst 4

Spiritual activities with others: Activities that happen largely outside of the organized church, such as spiritual friendships, evangelism, or serving those in need "on my own."

A catalyst is something that makes change happen.

A catalyst is something that makes change happen. Our analysis highlights the catalytic factors most influential to movement from one segment to the next on the spiritual continuum. In other words, out of the fifty factors included in the REVEAL survey, we want to identify those that seem to be most prevalent and significant as people move across the spiritual continuum. The focus of our discussion about these spiritual catalysts centers on three "movements"—the dynamic spaces between the segments on the spiritual continuum (chart 2-2).

Here is a brief overview of how the three movements relate to the four segments on the spiritual continuum.

Movement 1: The Earliest Stage of Spiritual Growth

In this movement, people gain their initial understanding of the Christian faith and accept that Jesus Christ offers the only path to salvation. They move from the Exploring Christ segment to the Growing in Christ segment.

Movement 2: The Intermediate Stage of Spiritual Growth

In this movement, people become more active in their personal spiritual experiences as they progress from the Growing in Christ segment to a more intimate Close to Christ relationship.

Chart 2-2: People progress across the spiritual continuum in three movements: Movement 1, early spiritual growth; Movement 2, intermediate spiritual growth; Movement 3, advanced spiritual growth.

Movement 3: The More Advanced Stage of Spiritual Growth

In this movement, a person's faith shifts from a daily awareness of Christ's presence and involvement (a Close to Christ relationship) to a redefinition of a person's identity based on their relationship with Christ (a Christ-Centered relationship).

It might be helpful to think of the three movements as stages of a learning experience. For example, Movement 1, the earliest learning stage, would be like grade school; Movement 2, high school; and Movement 3, college. The four categories of spiritual catalysts are something akin to subjects we learn in school—like math, which progresses from simple arithmetic in grade school, to algebra in high school and calculus in college. The subject of math is constant throughout the learning experience, but the kind of math students learn takes on different forms depending on where they are on the learning curve.

Chart 2-3: The colored bars illustrate the four major categories of spiritual catalysts that influence growth across the three movements.

Just as a progressive curriculum creates a learning path that moves from basic to more complex coursework, the three spiritual movements also progress from basic to more complex spiritual experiences. Each movement depends on the spiritual groundwork laid in the prior movement, just like high school academics build on fundamentals learned in grade school.

On the pages that follow, we evaluate four categories of spiritual catalysts (chart 2-3) so we can better understand which catalysts are most important at different points in the spiritual journey.

We start with spiritual beliefs and attitudes, since we find that a firm grounding in the core beliefs of Christianity is essential to all three movements on the spiritual continuum.

1. Spiritual Beliefs and Attitudes

Beliefs and attitudes reflect what we accept to be true or real. Beliefs can be straightforward, like those based exclusively on scientific fact; for example, we believe the world is round even though we can't see that for ourselves. Christian spiritual beliefs are different. They are less about believing in irrefutable data and more about accepting that a relationship with Jesus Christ is possible and desirable. In other words, spiritual beliefs are primarily centered on increasingly entrusting our lives to an ongoing relationship with Christ. In human terms, these beliefs are somewhat similar to decisions we make when we decide whether or not to lower our defenses by entrusting our heart to another person.

Beliefs and attitudes reflect what we accept to be true or real.

We measure spiritual beliefs and attitudes by asking people to express their agreement with core spiritual values (chart 2-4, page 32). On the chart, belief statements listed under each movement indicate that strong agreement with that belief is catalytic to growth in that movement. For example, belief in salvation by grace is a fundamental catalyst that moves people from the Exploring Christ segment to the Growing in Christ segment.

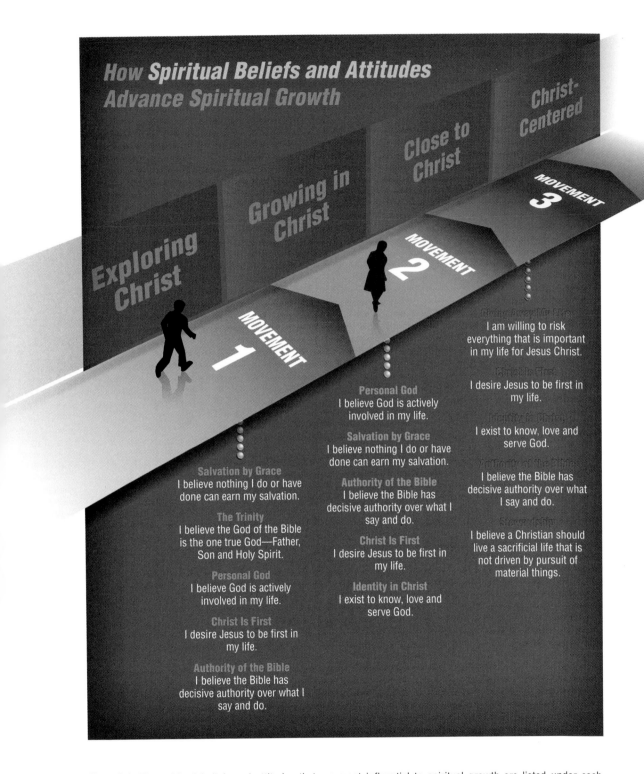

How *Spiritual Beliefs and Attitudes* Advance Spiritual Growth

Christ-Centered

Close to Christ

Growing in Christ

Exploring Christ

MOVEMENT 1

MOVEMENT 2

MOVEMENT 3

Movement 1

Salvation by Grace
I believe nothing I do or have done can earn my salvation.

The Trinity
I believe the God of the Bible is the one true God—Father, Son and Holy Spirit.

Personal God
I believe God is actively involved in my life.

Christ Is First
I desire Jesus to be first in my life.

Authority of the Bible
I believe the Bible has decisive authority over what I say and do.

Movement 2

Personal God
I believe God is actively involved in my life.

Salvation by Grace
I believe nothing I do or have done can earn my salvation.

Authority of the Bible
I believe the Bible has decisive authority over what I say and do.

Christ Is First
I desire Jesus to be first in my life.

Identity in Christ
I exist to know, love and serve God.

Movement 3

I am willing to risk everything that is important in my life for Jesus Christ.

Christ Is First
I desire Jesus to be first in my life.

Identity in Christ
I exist to know, love and serve God.

Authority of the Bible
I believe the Bible has decisive authority over what I say and do.

Stewardship
I believe a Christian should live a sacrificial life that is not driven by pursuit of material things.

Chart 2-4: The spiritual beliefs and attitudes that are most influential to spiritual growth are listed under each movement in order of importance.

To better explain how spiritual beliefs and attitudes function as catalysts, it's helpful to address the following three questions.

What does it mean that spiritual beliefs and attitudes are spiritual "catalysts"? Earlier, I described a catalyst as something that makes change happen. In the category of spiritual beliefs, this means that an increase in the intensity of a person's agreement with a belief statement—for example, belief in salvation by grace ("I strongly agree" or "very strongly agree that nothing I do or have done can earn my salvation")—is highly predictive of Movement 1, the early movement from Exploring Christ to Growing in Christ. Being "predictive" means we consistently see more people who "very strongly agree" with belief in salvation by grace when we compare people in the second segment (Growing in Christ) to the first segment (Exploring Christ). This leads us to identify salvation by grace as a catalytic factor that influences the movement of people from the first to the second segment (Movement 1).

Belief in salvation by grace is a catalytic factor that influences the movement of people from the first to the second segment.

Where do these statements come from? The eight belief and attitude statements on chart 2-4 are based on significant and recurring biblical themes. While there are many other beliefs and attitudes we could have chosen, these eight statements have consistently emerged in ongoing research on America's spiritual culture as the statements that best describe and define a person's spiritual condition (see "What Are the Spiritual Belief and Attitude Statements and Where Do They Come From?" on page 35).

Is the order of the statements significant? Yes, the statements are ranked from top to bottom in the order of their ability to influence movement. In this category of spiritual beliefs and attitudes, belief in salvation by grace is the most significant catalyst in Movement 1. Belief in the authority of the Bible is an important catalyst in this movement as well, but not as significant as the four statements that precede it.

Chart 2-4 is rich with insight about the beliefs and attitudes that must be strongly present for a person's heart to move from an early inquiry/exploration approach to faith, to being fully engaged as a committed Christ-follower. Here are two highlights from our analysis of this very important category.

The top-ranked statements tell a powerful story. On the path to becoming Christ-Centered, people must first be convinced of the fundamental truths of salvation by grace and the Trinity (Movement 1). Then they embrace belief in a personal God—a God who is "actively involved in my life" (Movement 2). This belief in God's omnipresence shifts to a strong desire for "Jesus to be first in my life" and a humble, heartfelt willingness to "risk everything that is important in my life for Jesus Christ" (Movement 3). This progression is a beautiful description of spiritual transformation, based empirically on thousands of responses from the hearts of God's people.

Two beliefs catalyze growth across all three movements. A desire for "Jesus to be first in my life" is a significant catalyst across all three movements, which means that this desire is increasingly embedded in the heart of a developing Christ-follower. A second important catalyst that appears consistently across all three movements is an increasing belief in the authority of the Bible.

A desire for "Jesus to be first in my life" is a significant catalyst across all three movements.

We know spiritual beliefs are catalytic to spiritual growth, but that begs two questions: Where do spiritual beliefs come from, and how are they formed and reinforced? Beyond the influence of family traditions, it's a fair assumption that the church undoubtedly plays a central role in shaping our first impressions of faith and introducing us to those foundational beliefs of the Trinity and salvation by grace. If the church is so central to inspiring and reinforcing spiritual growth, then which organized church activities are most instrumental? That is the focus of our next category: organized church activities.

Cally Parkinson

What Are the Spiritual Belief and Attitude Statements and Where Do They Come From?

THE PURPOSE OF OUR RESEARCH is to uncover insights about what advances spiritual growth and what gets in the way. Our working definition of spiritual growth is based on Christ's teaching about the greatest commandment—to love God and to love others (*Matthew 22:36–40*). In order to assess where people are spiritually, we used statements about spiritual beliefs and attitudes and asked them to describe how strongly they agreed with those statements.

Here are the statements we used:

- **Salvation by Grace:** "I believe nothing I do or have done can earn my salvation" (*Ephesians 2:8–9*).

- **The Trinity:** "I believe the God of the Bible is the one true God—Father, Son and Holy Spirit" (*2 Corinthians 13:14*).

- **Personal God:** "I believe God is actively involved in my life" (*Psalm 121*).

- **Christ Is First:** "I desire Jesus to be first in my life" (*Matthew 6:33*).

- **Authority of the Bible:** "I believe the Bible has decisive authority over what I say and do" (*2 Timothy 3:16–17*).

- **Identity in Christ:** "I exist to know, love and serve God" (*John 1:12–13*).

- **Stewardship:** "I believe a Christian should live a sacrificial life that is not driven by pursuit of material things" (*1 Timothy 6:17–19*).

- **Giving Away My Life:** "I am willing to risk everything that is important in my life for Jesus Christ" (*Romans 12:1–2*).

- **Giving Away My Faith:** "I pray for non-Christians to accept Jesus Christ as their Lord and Savior" (*Ephesians 6:19–20*).

- **Giving Away My Time:** "I give away my time to serve and help others in my community" (*Colossians 3:17*).

- **Giving Away My Money:** "My first priority in spending is to support God's work" (*2 Corinthians 8:7*).

These statements are based on Scripture and derived from the *Christian Life Profile Assessment Tool* created by Randy Frazee, senior minister of Oak Hills Community Church in San Antonio, Texas. Dozens of church leaders, theologians and others engaged in a rigorous process of biblical inquiry to find the core, repeatable characteristics of a follower of Christ. The statements were then tested and refined in multiple forums, including *The Spiritual State of the Union,* an ongoing benchmark of the "spiritual temperature" in America, sponsored by The University of Pennsylvania and The Gallup Organization. Among the experts contributing to this comprehensive effort were Dallas Willard, J. I. Packer and Larry Crabb. The thoroughness of this approach, as well as the caliber of people engaged in the process, prompted us to adopt these statements for use in our research. ◆

Statements were tested and refined in multiple forums.

2. Organized Church Activities

The church is the most significant organized influence on spiritual growth, so the activities of the church naturally emerge as important catalytic factors. Our latest research with over 200 churches reached the same conclusion about the role of the church as the research we did previously with only a handful of churches: *The catalytic power of the church is limited primarily to the first two movements of spiritual growth.* Also, the activity that commands most of the church's resources—weekend services—shows up as a significant catalyst only in Movement 1. It's important to point out that this finding comes from a database with a large percentage of churches (40 percent) that say they do not consider themselves seeker targeted or seeker friendly.

The catalytic power of the church is limited primarily to the first two movements of spiritual growth.

Chart 2-5 highlights our most recent findings, showing that traditional church activities are most influential in the first two movements of spiritual growth, with limited impact in the more advanced third movement.

Let's unpack this chart with three observations about the catalytic role of church activities across the spiritual continuum.

Weekend services appear to be catalytic to spiritual growth only in Movement 1. This is somewhat misleading because it implies that weekend attendance and satisfaction decline after Movement 1, and that's not the case. People attend weekend services at high rates in all three movements, and their satisfaction with the role of weekend services in their spiritual growth is also generally high. However, the greatest increase in participation occurs in the first movement of spiritual growth and then levels off. Satisfaction also plateaus after Movement 1. What does this mean?

It means that while weekend services are a primary source for spiritual "fuel," especially early in the journey, other church activities become increasingly important fueling stations as spiritual development progresses. Serving experiences and adult education classes on

continued on page 40

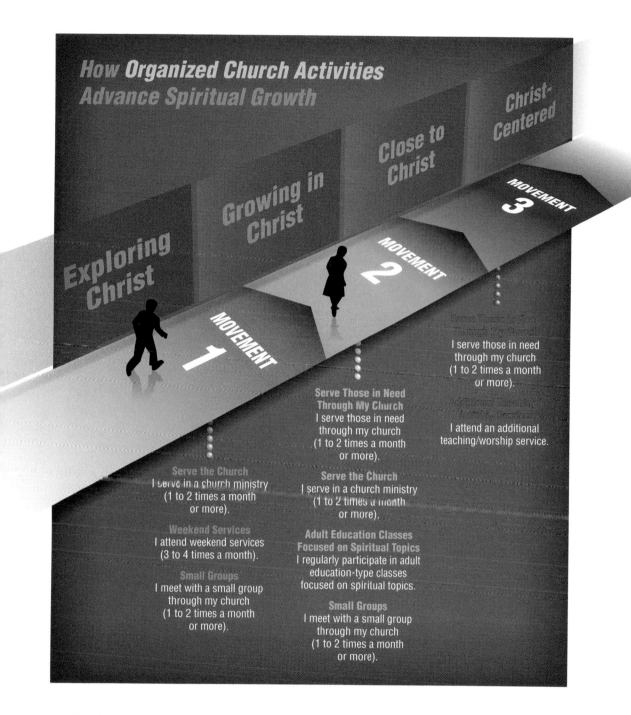

How Organized Church Activities Advance Spiritual Growth

Exploring Christ

Growing in Christ

Close to Christ

Christ-Centered

MOVEMENT 1

MOVEMENT 2

MOVEMENT 3

Serve Those in Need Through My Church
I serve those in need through my church (1 to 2 times a month or more).

Additional Teaching/Worship Service
I attend an additional teaching/worship service.

Serve Those in Need Through My Church
I serve those in need through my church (1 to 2 times a month or more).

Serve the Church
I serve in a church ministry (1 to 2 times a month or more).

Serve the Church
I serve in a church ministry (1 to 2 times a month or more).

Weekend Services
I attend weekend services (3 to 4 times a month).

Adult Education Classes Focused on Spiritual Topics
I regularly participate in adult education-type classes focused on spiritual topics.

Small Groups
I meet with a small group through my church (1 to 2 times a month or more).

Small Groups
I meet with a small group through my church (1 to 2 times a month or more).

Chart 2-5: The church activities that are most influential to spiritual growth are listed under each movement in order of importance.

Finding the (White Space)

IN THE MARKETPLACE, "finding the white space" is something of a holy grail. It refers to discovering unmet customer needs in advance of the competition. If you can create a product or service that meets those needs before anyone else, you capture the market. Is there a "white space" for the church's role in spiritual growth? For example, is there

What People Say They Need from the Church

What People Say They Need	Importance [1]	Satisfaction [2]	THE GAP [3]
Help me understand the Bible in depth.	87%	62%	25%
Help me develop a personal relationship with Christ.	86%	65%	21%
Provide strong programs for children.	85%	71%	14%
Challenge me to grow and take next steps.	83%	64%	19%
Provide compelling worship services.	80%	72%	8%
Help me in my time of emotional need.	75%	47%	28%
Help me feel like I belong.	73%	53%	20%
Provide opportunities to serve those in need.	68%	64%	4%
Provide opportunities to serve in ministry.	67%	69%	-2%
Help me to develop relationships that encourage accountability.	67%	39%	28%
Help me find a spiritual mentor.	50%	28%	22%

[1] Percentage of those who rated the statement "critically" or "very important" [2] Percentage of those who said they were "extremely" or "very satisfied" [3] Importance minus satisfaction

Chart 2-6: The 80,000 people surveyed rated eleven church attributes on importance to spiritual growth and satisfaction with how well the church met their expectations. Satisfaction was subtracted from importance to determine the biggest gaps, indicating areas of opportunity for church strategy.

an unmet need that, if addressed, could catapult people along the spiritual journey?

We looked through the research to see if there was evidence of people expressing unmet needs related to the church, which would mean they were experiencing a gap between what they'd like the church to deliver to help them grow spiritually, and what they actually receive.

Chart 2-6 shows how people responded when we asked them what they wanted most from their church, ranking eleven needs in order of importance and comparing people's satisfaction with how the church meets those needs in a gap analysis.

We found three important insights and white-space opportunities for the church.

1. The top five needs are the same for all three spiritual movements. Whether people are in the early, intermediate or more advanced stages of spiritual growth, the top five needs they express for the church are the same. These top five needs also rank well

above the other needs in every movement. And while the rank order might vary slightly by movement, "Help me understand the Bible in depth" is consistently at the top of the list.

2. The three biggest gaps are the same for all three movements. The circled numbers point to the biggest gaps between importance and satisfaction. This could be the white space in spiritual growth. The biggest gaps show up in "help me understand the Bible in depth," "help me in my time of emotional need," and "help me to develop relationships that encourage accountability." Importantly, these gaps exist across all three movements. This makes sense, since a need that is unmet early in the spiritual journey would likely persist from one stage to the next.

3. One of the biggest gaps is at the top of the importance rankings. It is significant that "help me understand the Bible in depth" shows up with one of the largest gaps between importance and satisfaction. It is the most important spiritual growth need expressed by people across the board, which, in a way, is good news. If the church can discover new and innovative ways to address this most significant gap, our research points to great kingdom gains as the result. ♦

spiritual topics are examples of the activities that advance spiritual development to higher levels, while the power of weekend services resides primarily early in the journey.

We do not mean to discount the significance of weekend services. In fact, as we note in chapter 4, weekend services are hugely important to achieving high levels of satisfaction with the church's role in spiritual growth. However, when it comes to measuring the catalysts most significant to spiritual growth (*not* satisfaction with the church), there are many other factors—like spiritual beliefs and attitudes, personal spiritual practices and spiritual activities happening largely outside of the church—that contribute in compelling ways. While weekend services are critically important, there are many other catalysts equally vital to spiritual heart change.

The top-ranked factors in all three movements include the word serve.

Serving is the most catalytic experience offered by the church. The top-ranked factors in all three movements include the word *serve*. That's very consistent with our spiritual growth trajectory being defined by an increasingly intimate relationship with Jesus Christ. Serving as his hands and feet, whether in a church ministry or serving those in need, seems to reinforce growth in that relationship. Interestingly, it appears that serving experiences are more significant to spiritual development than organized small groups, though small groups do show up as catalysts for the first two movements. But it's the serving experiences that demonstrate increasing levels of spiritual influence; and it's worth noting that serving those in need (versus serving in a church ministry) tops the list of catalysts for Movements 2 and 3.

Other church activities serve distinct purposes. "Adult education classes on spiritual topics" popped up as a significant catalyst in Movement 2. "Additional teaching/worship services," which were typically midweek services, also appeared as a catalytic church activity in Movement 3. Roughly half of the 200 churches had around 25 percent of people in their congregations report that they attend an "additional teaching/worship service."

This suggests that people in the intermediate and more advanced movements of spiritual growth benefit from church activities targeted to their needs. It also argues that a broader portfolio of church offerings might serve the mission of spiritual growth more effectively than a concentration of church resources in weekend services and small groups.

3. Personal Spiritual Practices

Personal spiritual practices are very powerful catalysts. We reached this conclusion in 2004 when the only church surveyed was Willow Creek, and our recent research with over 200 churches came to the same conclusion.

Chart 2-7 (page 42) shows the most influential spiritual practices for each spiritual movement. Chart 2-7 also demonstrates the analytical depth available to us in this expanded database. For example, instead of measuring only one dimension of prayer, like "daily prayer to seek guidance," we're able to assess the impact of this type of prayer going from occasional to frequent in Movement 1; then from frequent to daily in Movement 2. Being able to break down spiritual practices into multiple options of "rare, occasional, frequent and daily" allows us to identify the significance of the spiritual practices starting at the very beginning of spiritual development. This ability to look at people's spiritual practices in a more comprehensive way produced a number of new insights. We highlight two of them below.

"Reflection on Scripture" is the number one factor across all three movements. But that's only part of the story. When we statistically compare the power of these factors, "Reflection on Scripture" ("I reflect on the meaning of Scripture in my life") is much more influential than any other personal spiritual practice. In fact, for the most advanced segments—Close to Christ and Christ-Centered—it's twice as catalytic as any other factor. Using this same statistical comparison, daily prayer to seek guidance is a strong secondary spiritual practice, especially for Movement 2.

Many spiritual factors tested did not emerge as catalysts. Journaling, reading devotional materials and accessing Christian

"Reflection on Scripture" is more influential than any other personal spiritual practice.

materials outside of the church (listening to Christian music, radio or messages; reading Christian books; surfing Christian web sites) did not emerge as significant factors in the three spiritual growth

Chart 2-7: The personal spiritual practices that are most influential to spiritual growth are listed under each movement in order of importance.

movements. Compared with the factors highlighted on chart 2-7, these other activities did not predict movement nearly as well as the catalysts that emerged as most significant.

4. Spiritual Activities with Others

Spiritual activities with others take place largely outside the church and catalyze growth as people activate their faith through a variety of experiences. These activities include informal networks of spiritual friendships and confidants; evangelistic outreach; and serving those in need "on my own," which could mean serving through an organization like Habitat for Humanity, or simply helping out a neighbor who is going through a tough time.

Chart 2-8 (page 44) illustrates the spiritual activities with others that are most important to each movement of spiritual development.

The power of this category of catalysts is found in the human dynamics of the experiences. Each factor involves some risk—like the risk of going public with one's faith through evangelism, or exposing spiritual shortfalls to another believer. Building faith privately through personal spiritual practices or within the safe confines of the church are relatively easy roads compared to the public displays involved in these catalysts. But taking risk builds faith, and we can see an increasing risk level in the catalysts that emerge across the three movements.

Here are two key insights about spiritual activities with others.

Spiritual community is a critical catalyst for spiritual growth. Spiritual community shows up as a growth catalyst in all three movements, though its form shifts from more casual friendships to mentor relationships, implying more accountability and more risk. The role of spiritual friendships in the first two movements coincides with the role of small groups on chart 2-5 (page 37), which isn't surprising. It would seem logical that many spiritual friendships begin with an organized church activity like small groups or serving.

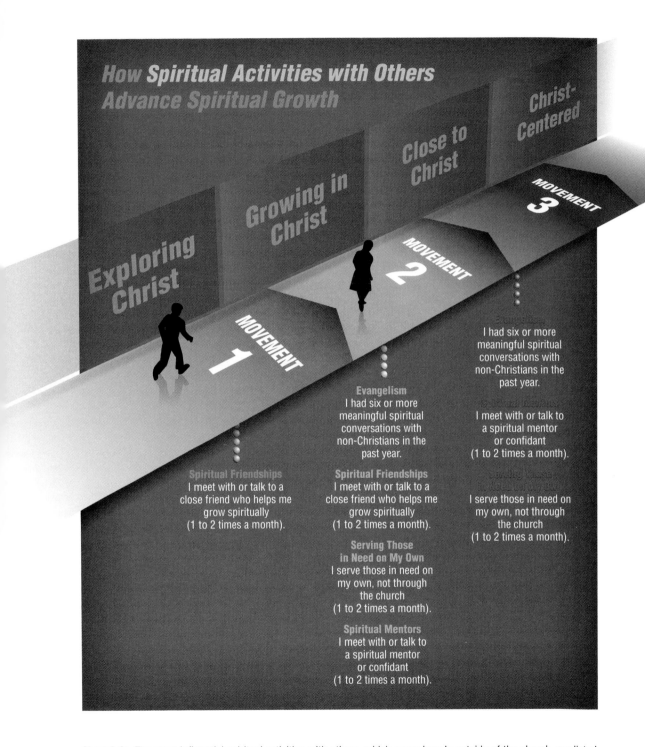

How *Spiritual Activities with Others* Advance Spiritual Growth

Exploring Christ

Growing in Christ

Close to Christ

Christ-Centered

MOVEMENT 1

MOVEMENT 2

MOVEMENT 3

Spiritual Friendships
I meet with or talk to a close friend who helps me grow spiritually
(1 to 2 times a month).

Evangelism
I had six or more meaningful spiritual conversations with non-Christians in the past year.

Spiritual Friendships
I meet with or talk to a close friend who helps me grow spiritually
(1 to 2 times a month).

Serving Those in Need on My Own
I serve those in need on my own, not through the church
(1 to 2 times a month).

Spiritual Mentors
I meet with or talk to a spiritual mentor or confidant
(1 to 2 times a month).

Evangelism
I had six or more meaningful spiritual conversations with non-Christians in the past year.

Spiritual Mentors
I meet with or talk to a spiritual mentor or confidant
(1 to 2 times a month).

Serving Those in Need on My Own
I serve those in need on my own, not through the church
(1 to 2 times a month).

Chart 2-8: The most influential spiritual activities with others, which occur largely outside of the church, are listed under each movement in order of their importance to advancing spiritual growth.

It is important to note that when people were asked which type of spiritual community is most important to advancing their spiritual growth, everyone chose spiritual friendships (chart 2-9).

All Segments Say Spiritual Friendships Are
Their Most Important Source of Spiritual Community

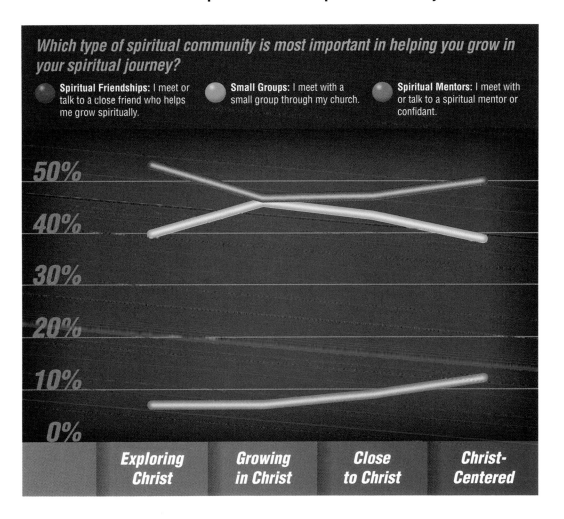

Which type of spiritual community is most important in helping you grow in your spiritual journey?

Spiritual Friendships: I meet or talk to a close friend who helps me grow spiritually.

Small Groups: I meet with a small group through my church.

Spiritual Mentors: I meet with or talk to a spiritual mentor or confidant.

50%
40%
30%
20%
10%
0%

| Exploring Christ | Growing in Christ | Close to Christ | Christ-Centered |

Chart 2-9: The highest percentage of people in each segment said that spiritual friendships are their most important source of spiritual community, compared with small groups and spiritual mentors.

This is a significant insight because many churches operate under the assumption that everyone should be in an organized form of spiritual community, like small groups or serving. Our research suggests that it's very important for churches to encourage formal, organized gatherings—like small groups and serving experiences—but it's also okay for people to let go of the organized structure at some point. A key output of the organized structure is to allow powerful informal relational networks to develop, which implies that the role of the organized structure may be temporary.

We hypothesize that evangelism is both a cause and an effect.

This is consistent with the evidence that relationships designed for spiritual accountability, like mentors/confidants, would be welcomed by people in the intermediate and more advanced spiritual movements. The average small group size of six to twelve is inconsistent with an intimate accountability relationship, which, by definition, is more likely to occur in the context of a one-on-one relationship.

Evangelism is the most catalytic factor for Movements 2 and 3. This raises the question of whether evangelism is a "cause" or "effect." In other words, is evangelism simply an output, an effect of a growing faith? Or is evangelism (defined as "having six or more meaningful conversations with non-Christians a year") a cause of spiritual growth—a catalytic experience in itself, growing the heart of a Christ-follower who engages in dialogue with a non-believer?

Our Conclusion . . .

From the research we can only conclude that higher levels of evangelism are highly predictive of spiritual growth in the intermediate and advanced movements. We hypothesize that evangelism is *both* a cause and an effect. It emerges from a believer's heart as an output, so it is an effect; but it is also a cause of spiritual growth as it reenergizes and reinforces a believer's faith.

SPIRITUAL GROWTH— IS IT LINEAR?

After all of the data and discussion about empirical findings, it may appear that we believe spiritual growth is a step-by-step, linear process. However, nothing could be further from the truth.

Spiritual growth is a highly individual process, full of mysterious moments that crystallize and catalyze our faith. There is no clear pattern of stepping stones that guarantees spiritual maturity. In fact, most of us would likely say we've experienced more twists and turns than straightforward progress in our spiritual journeys.

The image of a "spiritual orchestra" might help to reconcile the mystery of spiritual growth with our data-driven research findings and charts.

If you've ever attended a musical theater production or a symphony, you've listened to an orchestra playing music using four different kinds of instruments:

> **Woodwinds— clarinet, oboe, bassoon, etc.**
>
> **Strings— violin, viola, bass, etc.**
>
> **Brass— trumpet, trombone, tuba, etc.**
>
> **Percussion— snare drum, cymbals, timpani, etc.**

Throughout an orchestra performance, all the instruments remain on stage, even when they aren't playing. For example, the percussion instruments might play for only a few moments in a given piece, but they stay in place. The instruments may be silent from time to time, but they are never absent. And when they do play, their sound can be muted or magnified depending on the movement of the music.

Think about the four groups of spiritual catalysts like these four groups of musical instruments. Like the orchestra instruments that never leave during a performance, our four categories of spiritual

There is no clear pattern of stepping stones that guarantees spiritual maturity.

catalysts never leave the spiritual "stage." They are always present and active in a person's spiritual development—though their impact and influence on spiritual growth varies, in some cases, dramatically, across the three movements along the spiritual continuum. Like the movements in a symphony, these spiritual movements are quite distinct. But they flow from one to another, using the same "instruments" (catalysts) to build the spiritual headway necessary to advance to the next level.

How many different musical pieces could be played using the four groups of instruments in the orchestra? Hundreds? Thousands? Maybe millions? Similarly, how many spiritual journeys could be crafted using different combinations of beliefs, church activities, spiritual practices and spiritual activities with others? Many, many more than we can imagine. Just as music is written with countless combinations of chords and tones, so too are spiritual journeys written with unique imprints from a divine hand.

The spiritual journey is unique for each individual.

So the four groups of spiritual catalysts remain on stage, but the spiritual journey is unique for each individual. The research tells us about the general role and importance of over fifty catalysts in the spiritual movements. But the mystery remains in the individual pattern of the spiritual pathway—everyone's spiritual symphony is unique.

STRIKE UP THE BAND!

We now understand how the four categories of catalysts move across the spiritual continuum. If we threw all fifty-plus catalysts into the same spiritual pot, which ones do you think would emerge as the most important factors in spiritual growth? Would it be spiritual beliefs and attitudes? How about personal spiritual practices? What about spiritual activities with others? Out of all of the factors, which are most important to Movement 1? Movement 2? Movement 3?

That's what's next. It's time to "strike up the band" and look at each spiritual movement individually to see which factors are the most powerful catalysts of all across the spiritual continuum.

CALLY PARKINSON

3 THE
SPIRITUAL
GROWTH
LEARNING
CURVE

THE KEY DRIVERS OF SPIRITUAL GROWTH

growth

SPIRITUAL GROWTH NEEDS ARE dramatically different for early believers compared to committed Christ-followers. What does and does not inspire growth at different stages of spiritual development? We dive deep into the research to find out.

③

THE SPIRITUAL GROWTH LEARNING CURVE

Learning is not a one-dimensional process. People gain knowledge and skills through multiple inputs—from classroom teaching and study, to hands-on training and experiences. A good example is a medical student who studies complex principles of chemistry, utilizes those principles in college lab experiments and then applies them in practical ways to patients as a medical intern.

Spiritual growth shares the complexity of this multidimensional learning curve; people grow spiritually through multiple inputs—from teaching and study, to spiritual coaching and everyday spiritual experiences. We reviewed the sources of those inputs in chapter 2 (catalysts such as spiritual beliefs and attitudes, church activities, etc.), but we looked at them *horizontally* as though they were independent categories. This is akin to evaluating a student's learning progress by looking at academic performance in just one subject, like math.

The purpose of this chapter is to unpack the complexity of the spiritual growth learning curve by looking at how all the categories of spiritual catalysts come together and influence each of the three spiritual movements. In other words, we'll take a *vertical* approach and dive deeply into each spiritual movement, focusing on which catalysts are most influential for each one (chart 3-1).

People grow spiritually through multiple inputs—from teaching and study, to spiritual coaching and everyday spiritual experiences.

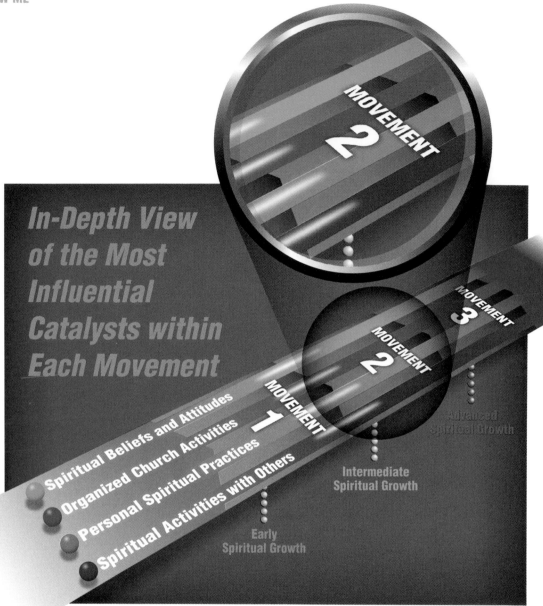

In-Depth View of the Most Influential Catalysts within Each Movement

Spiritual Beliefs and Attitudes
Organized Church Activities
Personal Spiritual Practices
Spiritual Activities with Others

MOVEMENT 1
Early Spiritual Growth

MOVEMENT 2
Intermediate Spiritual Growth

MOVEMENT 3
Advanced Spiritual Growth

Chart 3-1: The magnified view of Movement 2 illustrates that in this chapter we focus on the most important spiritual growth catalysts for each of the three spiritual movements.

Taking this deeper look at each movement enables us to identify the key factors that are most predictive of spiritual growth. This language of "predictability" refers to the combination of factors that most often cause a certain outcome. For example, the combination of high blood pressure, high cholesterol and being overweight tends to predict a poor heart condition. When we say certain spiritual factors are "more predictive" than others, it means that when such factors are present, spiritual growth is more likely to occur; just like a poor heart condition is more likely to occur when a patient is overweight and also has high blood pressure and high cholesterol. Predictability is what this chapter is all about—identifying the factors that are most predictive of spiritual growth.

Based on our analysis of more than fifty spiritual catalysts, we rank the most predictive factors in order of importance for each spiritual growth movement, and we also show how much more important one factor is compared to another. To illustrate why this concept is so critical, let's consider how ranking works in another familiar category—favorite ice cream flavors.

What's your favorite ice cream flavor?

If it's vanilla, you're in good company. Vanilla is number one on the list of the ten most popular ice cream flavors. Chocolate is number two, then strawberry and on down the list. But there is a flaw in this ranking. The ranking itself is correct, but it's misleading as an indicator of vanilla's real popularity. Vanilla not only ranks number one; it's also twice as popular as chocolate. And chocolate is significantly more popular than any other flavor on the top-ten list.

When it comes to identifying and ranking factors that catalyze spiritual growth, we're looking for the spiritual equivalent of vanilla. We want to know the order of importance for the factors influencing growth in each of the three movements, but we also want to know if any factors stand out. These vanilla-type factors deserve attention and resources because they represent spiritual catalysts that have greater power and influence than others—the kind of catalysts with the potential for exponential impact on spiritual growth.

Every church has limited time and resources. Our hope is that by identifying the highest impact catalysts for each spiritual growth movement, we can shed light on which ministry efforts are the most deserving of our time and attention.

When it comes to identifying and ranking factors that catalyze spiritual growth, we're looking for the spiritual equivalent of vanilla.

MOVEMENT 1: ALL ABOUT FUNDAMENTALS

Learning something new—like how to play a sport or a musical instrument, or how to speak another language—always begins with a good grasp of the fundamentals. Movement 1 represents the earliest stage of spiritual development on the continuum, so—not surprisingly—the most important spiritual catalysts are activities and practices critical to developing the fundamentals of Christian faith (chart 3-2).

Learning something new always begins with a good grasp of the fundamentals.

**The Most Influential Catalysts
for Movement 1**

Moving from Exploring Christ to Growing in Christ	
Spiritual Beliefs and Attitudes	Salvation by Grace The Trinity Personal God Christ Is First Authority of the Bible
Church Activities	Serve the Church Weekend Services Small Groups
Personal Spiritual Practices	Reflection on Scripture (*rare to frequent*) Bible Reading (*rare to frequent*) Prayer to Seek Guidance (*occasional to frequent*) Prayer to Confess Sins
Spiritual Activities with Others	Spiritual Friendships

Chart 3-2: These are the most important factors from each one of the four categories of spiritual catalysts for Movement 1.

Out of more than fifty factors, the thirteen factors on chart 3-2 emerged as most important to catalyzing spiritual growth in Movement 1. In terms of a spiritual growth learning curve, the activities and experiences in Movement 1 share interesting similarities with the grade school years.

Grade school is a time when we grapple with the fundamentals of spelling and arithmetic. We experience our first social structures with classes and activity groups, and those structures produce many of our first friendships. We learn how to interact in large group settings and how to read on our own. This is a time filled with the excitement of new discoveries and coming to terms with who we are beyond the family circle.

Similar new experiences and discoveries characterize the spiritual growth of people in Movement 1. They wrestle with foundational Christian beliefs and begin to participate in organized church structures, such as serving and small groups, that produce enduring spiritual friendships. They also take their first steps toward biblical literacy, reflection on Scripture and prayer—practices that will sustain them on their journey across the spiritual continuum.

Spiritual growth of individuals in Movement 1 is characterized by wrestling with foundational Christian beliefs.

Two key insights

The following two key insights about Movement 1 focus on the high importance of foundational beliefs for these early believers, and the "on ramp" role played by the church for their first spiritual growth experiences.

Foundational Beliefs Are Critical

The dictionary defines belief as "acceptance by the mind that something is true or real, often underpinned by an emotional or spiritual sense of certainty." Without full acceptance in the belief that salvation by grace and the Trinity are true, it is difficult to imagine experiencing authentic spiritual growth as a Christian. So it is not surprising that the spiritual growth of individuals in Movement 1 is characterized by wrestling with foundational Christian beliefs. Chart 3-3 shows the surge in agreement with these beliefs that occurs between the Exploring Christ and Growing in Christ segments.

Building Beliefs Is Crucial for Those in the Early Segments of Spiritual Growth

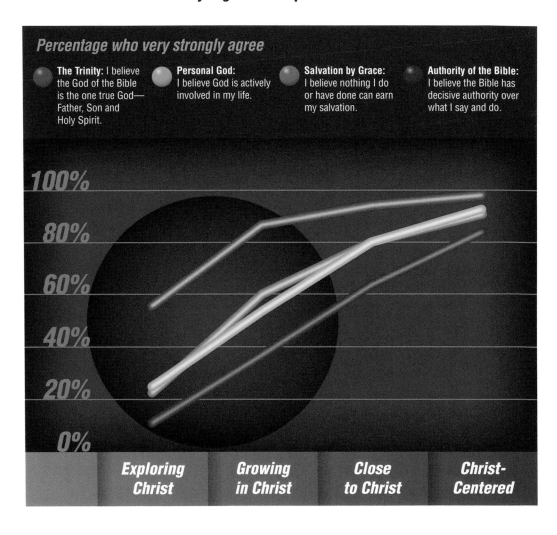

Percentage who very strongly agree

The Trinity: I believe the God of the Bible is the one true God—Father, Son and Holy Spirit.

Personal God: I believe God is actively involved in my life.

Salvation by Grace: I believe nothing I do or have done can earn my salvation.

Authority of the Bible: I believe the Bible has decisive authority over what I say and do.

100%
80%
60%
40%
20%
0%

| Exploring Christ | Growing in Christ | Close to Christ | Christ-Centered |

Chart 3-3: The steep increases (circled) in the percentage of people who "very strongly agree" with four core Christian beliefs show that establishing beliefs is a significant influence to movement from Exploring Christ to Growing in Christ.

Perhaps there is nothing more important to a person's ultimate conversion to the Christian faith, and even to the pace and depth of their spiritual growth over a lifetime, than to fully understand and accept the implications of these core beliefs. These spiritual fundamentals are as critical to spiritual growth as basic arithmetic is to learning calculus, or the rules of grammar are to writing a thesis. The church provides an essential learning platform for these fundamental beliefs as well as a faith-based environment for a person's early impressions of Christian life.

Church activities are crucial to providing social structures for early believers.

Church Activities Provide an "On Ramp" to Spiritual Growth

Church activities form the most critical "on ramp" for the development and reinforcement of spiritual beliefs and attitudes. Church activities are also crucial to providing social structures for early believers so that spiritual friendships and other relationships can form. The church plays its most vital role in Movement 1 when people are first dipping their toes into the waters of Christian faith and practice. The church's ability to provide an on ramp to spiritual growth is evident in the significant increase in participation in three church activities between the Exploring Christ and Growing in Christ segments (chart 3-4).

Participation in Church Activities Increases Significantly for Those in the Early Segments of Spiritual Growth

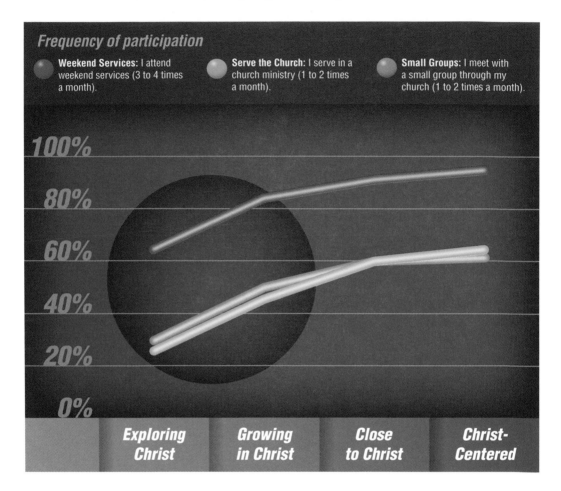

Chart 3-4: The sizeable increases (circled) in the percentage of people who participate in church activities show that a growing connection with the church is a significant influence to movement from Exploring Christ to Growing in Christ.

The church functions as a spiritual classroom for these early believers. It offers a protected, nurturing environment that provides reinforcement for the development of beliefs; and it provides opportunities to experience faith in community (small groups) and faith in action (serving). The fact that participation levels flatten in later stages of spiritual development suggests that more advanced growth is inspired by additional factors beyond church activities. Even the weekend service, which plateaus at a very high participation level, gets its biggest lift—and, consequently, has its greatest catalytic impact—in the earliest segments. We'll give more attention to this in chapter 4, which unpacks the importance of people's satisfaction with the role of weekend services in their spiritual growth.

The Top Five Spiritual Catalysts for Movement 1

Chart 3-5 shows the rank order of the five factors most predictive of spiritual growth in Movement 1. As noted earlier, the greatest need in this movement is to build a firm foundation of Christian beliefs. This is affirmed by the fact that the two most important spiritual growth catalysts are beliefs: salvation by grace and the Trinity.

The two most important spiritual growth catalysts are beliefs: salvation by grace and the Trinity.

Movement 1:
From Exploring Christ to Growing in Christ

The Top Five Catalysts Influencing Movement 1*

1. **Salvation by Grace** (Spiritual Belief / Attitude)

2. **The Trinity** (Spiritual Belief / Attitude)

3. **Serve the Church** (Church Activity)

4. **Prayer to Seek Guidance** (Spiritual Practice)

5. **Reflection on Scripture** (Spiritual Practice)

* Listed in order of importance. See appendix 2, "Research Approach and Methodology" (page 144), for a more detailed explanation of the statistical approach used for analysis.

Chart 3-5: The top five spiritual catalysts out of the more than fifty factors evaluated are listed in order of importance for Movement 1. These five factors represent the combination of catalysts that are most predictive of movement from Exploring Christ to Growing in Christ.

A rock-solid belief in salvation by grace is the most influential factor in Movement 1.

Belief in salvation by grace is the number one catalyst, but is it a vanilla factor—something that truly stands head and shoulders above the other five factors? Our answer is a qualified "yes." It's qualified because belief in salvation by grace is most predictive of movement from the Exploring Christ segment to the Growing in Christ segment by a good margin, but it's not a huge margin. It is 20 percent more predictive than belief in the Trinity, and 50 percent more predictive than the other three factors. This means that a rock-solid belief in salvation by grace ("I very strongly agree that nothing I do or have done can earn my salvation") is the most influential factor in Movement 1, but its influence is not two times greater than the second factor (belief in the Trinity), which is our vanilla yardstick.

This significance of foundational beliefs in Movement 1 makes total sense. After all, it is in Movement 1 that people make the decision to accept Christ as Lord and Savior. It is also interesting that taking the first steps into personal spiritual practices through prayer and reflection on Scripture shows up as more important to spiritual growth than the other factors in our analysis. This means that encouraging people to engage in personal spiritual practices is catalytic (it makes change happen). Reflecting back on the grade school analogy, this could be somewhat similar to our earliest experiences with reading and math, when we first realized we could decipher a pathway of learning on our own, independent of our parents or the teacher. Likewise, in Movement 1, these initial forays into spiritual practices are the first steps toward building a more personal—versus church-centric—relationship with Christ, and they appear to be very catalytic to early spiritual growth.

Serving in a church ministry is the most influential church activity in Movement 1. The reason for this may be twofold. First, serving provides a real-life opportunity for an active, faith-based experience, stepping beyond the more passive activity of attending weekend services. It makes faith come alive, which could be why it is more catalytic to growth than other church activities. The second reason serving is so influential relates to the last item on chart 3-2 (page 54), which is the importance of spiritual friendships. Serving in a church ministry may be the best strategy to meet relational needs for those in the first stages of spiritual growth. This relational connection could be what makes the serving experience especially catalytic. These two characteristics of serving—the active nature of the experience and its community-based setting—may explain why our analysis shows that serving in a church ministry is the most influential church activity.

Movement 1 is about the fundamentals . . .

Movement 1 is about the fundamentals of Christian beliefs and taking the first steps toward creating an active, personal faith. Let's recall the implications of those top five most predictive catalytic factors. Just as high blood pressure, high cholesterol and being overweight are predictive of a poor heart condition, these five factors are most predictive of spiritual growth in Movement 1. While all the factors on chart 3-2 are important to spiritual growth for early believers, these top five are the ones to target for maximum spiritual growth impact.

MOVEMENT 2: PRACTICE, PRACTICE, PRACTICE

Once a person demonstrates a solid grasp of the fundamentals, all good coaches and teachers have the same timeworn advice: *Practice!* The more you play an instrument, or practice jump shots, or immerse yourself in a new language, the more likely you are to truly master the skill.

This concept of practice is a central theme of Movement 2. Eighteen factors emerged as catalysts for this movement (chart 3-6, page 62). In this movement, spiritual growth goes from a beginner level, when a person is first Growing in Christ, to an intermediate level of Close to Christ intimacy. What we see is evidence of increased immersion (practice) in the activities and relationships that advance spiritual growth to deeper levels of personal conviction and devotion to Christ.

This concept of practice is a central theme of Movement 2.

**The Most Influential Catalysts
for Movement 2**

Greater independence, increased complexity and deepening relationships characterize spiritual growth in Movement 2.

Moving from Growing in Christ to Close to Christ	
Spiritual Beliefs and Attitudes	Personal God Salvation by Grace Authority of the Bible Christ Is First Identity in Christ
Church Activities	Serve the Church Serve Those in Need Through My Church Adult Education Classes on Spiritual Topics Small Groups
Personal Spiritual Practices	Prayer to Seek Guidance (*frequent to daily*) Reflection on Scripture (*frequent*) Tithing Solitude Bible Reading (*frequent*)
Spiritual Activities with Others	Evangelism Spiritual Friendships Serving Those in Need on My Own Spiritual Mentors

Chart 3-6: These are the most important factors from each one of the four categories of spiritual catalysts for Movement 2.

The learning curve analogy might offer additional insight into what happens in Movement 2, which is akin to the high school years. This season of a student's life is typically characterized by increasing independence—more homework and studying on one's own, away from the support of school and teachers. It is also characterized by increased complexity—going to a more diverse curriculum that includes sciences and history along with more complicated levels of math and literature. Social relationships also deepen and become an increasingly important source of advice and counsel on life's challenges and crossroads.

Greater independence, increased complexity and deepening relationships also characterize spiritual growth in Movement 2. We see the increased independence in the longer list of catalytic personal spiritual practices as people take on more personal responsibility for their spiritual growth. We see the increased complexity in their choice of church activities such as adult education classes and serving those in need. Deepening relationships show up with the addition of spiritual mentors along with spiritual friendships as catalytic relationships; and also in outreach activities, like evangelism and serving those in need on my own, as people begin to respond to Christ's love of the lost and the disenfranchised.

Looking over this list of catalytic factors, it's easy to see the increased level of spiritual engagement in Movement 2. The most dominant force driving this spiritual engagement is a routine practice of spiritual disciplines that feeds an active, personal and intimate relationship with Christ. This shift—from the more passive, dependent-on-the-church relationship with Christ of Movement 1— to a more active, personal, Close to Christ relationship, is the biggest insight for spiritual growth in Movement 2.

Faith Shifts from Passive to Active

In Movement 1, people allow the church to carry much of the responsibility for their spiritual development; in Movement 2, that scenario changes radically. People take on much more responsibility for their spiritual growth as they come to grips with the truth that a personal God is actively present and involved in their daily life experiences (chart 3-7).

The most dominant force driving spiritual engagement is a routine practice of spiritual disciplines.

In Movement 2, people shift their relationship with Jesus Christ from one of detached admiration to an experience of ongoing communication and intimacy. Think about someone you like and respect whom you may see perhaps once a week at work or when you take a walk

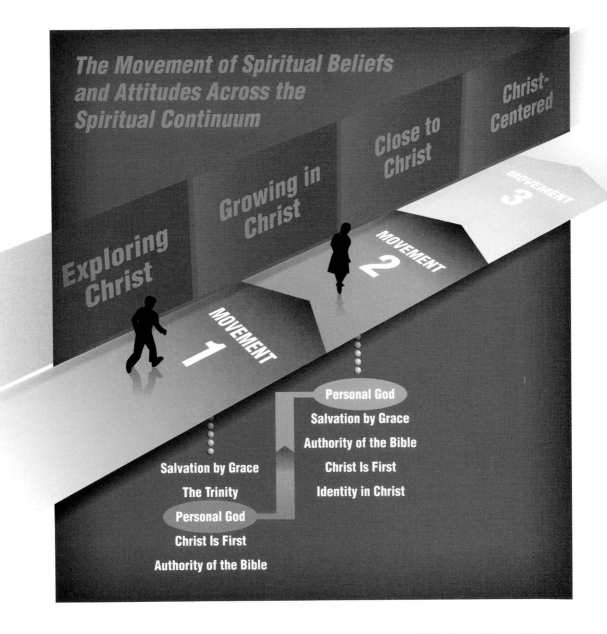

The Movement of Spiritual Beliefs and Attitudes Across the Spiritual Continuum

Exploring Christ

Growing in Christ

Close to Christ

Christ-Centered

MOVEMENT 1

MOVEMENT 2

MOVEMENT 3

Personal God
Salvation by Grace
Authority of the Bible
Christ Is First
Identity in Christ

Salvation by Grace
The Trinity
Personal God
Christ Is First
Authority of the Bible

Chart 3-7: Belief in a personal God ("I believe God is actively involved in my life") rises to the most important spiritual belief catalyst in Movement 2 compared with third-most-important catalyst in Movement 1.

through your neighborhood. Now think about a trusted friend—someone intimately familiar with you and your circumstances; someone you would contact immediately if faced with a crisis. The respected acquaintance and the intimate friend are two very different relationships. In Movement 2, people move from a more passive, once-a-week type of encounter, to an almost daily experience of personal interactions. And those personal interactions are fed by a significant increase in spiritual practices.

People move from a more passive, once-a-week type of encounter, to an almost daily experience of personal interactions.

Personal Spiritual Practices Become a Part of Life

The deepest, most trustworthy relationships in our lives grow as a direct result of the time and energy we put into them. Those investments take many forms—like hours of conversations, or messages of encouragement and support or a comforting presence in a dark time. People in Movement 2 accelerate the frequency of these types of investments in their relationship with God. We see big increases in personal spiritual practices—like daily prayer and Bible study—between the Growing in Christ and Close to Christ segments (chart 3.8, page 66)

It makes sense that increasing the frequency of time and energy spent in communication with God pays off in an increasingly intimate relationship with him. But what is more subtle, and perhaps more significant, is the increasing two-way nature of the relationship. It's not just *talking* to God that's important; it's also *listening* to God and receiving answers to prayer that is vital. It's not just reading the Bible that spurs spiritual growth; it is reflecting on the meaning of Scripture in a way that changes how a person thinks and lives that proves most significant.

This two-way street builds throughout Movement 2, creating a spiritual relationship characterized by a regular back-and-forth between the individual and God that facilitates a flow of encouragement, gratitude, insight, guidance and support. This is when the intellectually based relationship of Movement 1—rooted in facts about God—transforms into an emotionally rich relationship *with* God.

Personal Spiritual Practices Increase Between the Growing in Christ and Close to Christ Segments

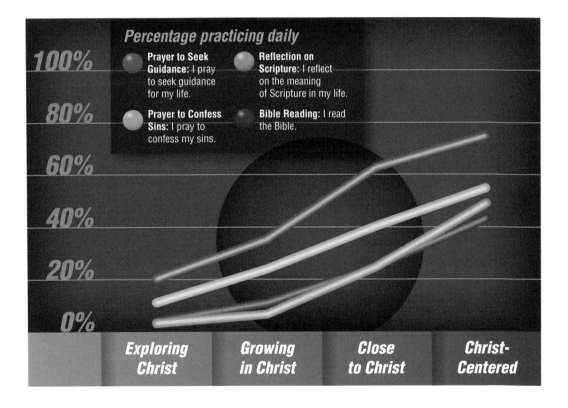

Chart 3-8: The steep increases (circled) in the percentage of people reporting daily spiritual practices shows that establishing a regular routine of spiritual disciplines is a significant influence to movement from Growing in Christ to Close to Christ.

The Top Five Spiritual Catalysts for Movement 2

The top five most predictive catalysts for Movement 2 affirm that this intermediate level of spiritual growth is characterized by an increasingly personal relationship with Jesus Christ fed by a menu of regular spiritual practices (chart 3-9). Belief in a personal God is the top catalyst, followed by three spiritual practices. While believing in a personal God is the most predictive factor for this movement, it does not rise to the level of a vanilla influence because the next two factors—prayer to seek guidance and reflection on Scripture—follow closely behind. The spiritual practice of solitude is also important but not nearly as significant as the first three catalysts.

Evangelism appears as the fifth catalyst, which foreshadows what we'll see in Movement 3. When people express higher levels of engagement with personal spiritual practices and higher levels of agreement with spiritual beliefs and attitudes, such as "I exist to know, love and serve God," it's logical to assume we'll see higher

Movement 2:
From Growing in Christ to Close to Christ

The Top Five Catalysts Influencing Movement 2*

1. **Personal God** (Spiritual Belief / Attitude)

2. **Prayer to Seek Guidance** (Spiritual Practice)

3. **Reflection on Scripture** (Spiritual Practice)

4. **Solitude** (Spiritual Practice)

5. **Evangelism** (Spiritual Activity with Others)

* Listed in order of importance. See appendix 2, "Research Approach and Methodology" (page 144), for a more detailed explanation of the statistical approach used for analysis.

This intermediate level of spiritual growth is characterized by an increasingly personal relationship with Jesus Christ.

Chart 3-9: The top five spiritual catalysts out of the more than fifty factors evaluated are listed in order of importance for Movement 2. These five factors represent the combination of catalysts that are most predictive of movement from Growing in Christ to Close to Christ.

levels of spiritual behaviors—like evangelism and serving the poor—as expressions of increasing faith. That's why it's not surprising to see evangelism among the top five catalysts for Movement 2, since this movement is characterized by high levels of both spiritual beliefs and personal spiritual practices.

As with Movement 1, it's good to think of these five factors as the conditions that are most likely to create a certain outcome. So these are the five factors most predictive of spiritual growth in Movement 2, and the ones to target for maximum impact at this intermediate level of spiritual development.

It is hard to over-estimate the importance of establishing a daily rhythm and routine of spiritual practices.

Fed by frequent prayer, reflection on Scripture and other spiritual practices, the people in this movement are growing toward an increasingly intimate relationship with God. They would welcome Bible studies, classes on spiritual topics and retreats because spiritual practices loom so large as the building blocks shaping and inspiring their growth. It is hard to overestimate the importance of establishing a daily rhythm and routine of spiritual practices in Movement 2, not only because of the impact on spiritual growth but also because it sets the stage for the outpouring of faith-based activity we see in Movement 3.

MOVEMENT 3: IN THE ZONE

On the learning curve of any new skill there is a sweet spot when fundamentals and practice finally pay off. It's called being "in the zone." Chicago Bulls' legend Michael Jordan provides a great example. When Jordan was in the zone, he rarely missed a shot, no matter what the opposition did to try and stop him. In one championship playoff game, he hit six out of six three-point shots in the first half and capped this feat with his famous shrug to the audience. Even he seemed mystified by his performance.

Those in the Christ-Centered segment are "in the zone" for the kingdom. They have internalized the fundamentals of Christian belief, and personal spiritual practices are as routine as brushing their teeth. Christ-Centered behavior pours out of them because of their passionate faith.

The important catalysts for Movement 3 paint a picture of Christ-followers who are greatly inspired by their faith (chart 3-10). Their number one spiritual attitude is "giving away my life," which means they strongly agree that "I am willing to surrender all that is important in my life to Jesus Christ." Serving those in need leads the list of

The Most Influential Catalysts
for Movement 3

Moving from Close to Christ to Christ-Centered	
Spiritual Beliefs and Attitudes	Giving Away My Life
	Christ Is First
	Identity in Christ
	Authority of the Bible
	Stewardship
Church Activities	Serve Those in Need Through My Church
	Additional Teaching / Worship Service
	Serve the Church
Personal Spiritual Practices	Reflection on Scripture (*frequent to daily*)
	Solitude (*occasional to daily*)
	Bible Reading (*frequent to daily*)
	Prayer to Seek Guidance & Confess Sins (*daily*)
	Tithing
Spiritual Activities with Others	Evangelism
	Spiritual Mentors
	Serving Those in Need on My Own

Those in the Christ-Centered segment are "in the zone" for the kingdom.

Chart 3-10: These are the most important factors from each one of the four categories of spiritual catalysts for Movement 3.

important church activities, along with additional teaching services and serving at the church. Their personal spiritual practices shift full throttle to activities experienced daily rather than frequently or occasionally. And their spiritual connections with others expand through increased evangelism, mentor relationships and serving those in need.

People in Movement 3 are characterized by a sense of individual responsibility similar to students in the college years. In college, students are on their own, making moral choices without parental oversight, as well as independent decisions about coursework and relationships that will significantly influence the trajectory of their lives.

They put their deep passion for Jesus Christ into action through evangelism, serving the poor and encouraging others.

Believers in Movement 3 are marked by a similar sense of spiritual responsibility in their passionate commitment to follow Christ's call on their lives. They do not rely on external influences for spiritual motivation and direction, and they make the kind of ethical and moral choices required to pursue their Christ-Centered commitment without compromise, rejecting alternative paths. They put their deep passion for Jesus Christ into action through evangelism, serving the poor and encouraging others. All of these behaviors emerge from a love for Christ that defines their identity. That's why we suggest that those who are growing in this movement are spiritually in the zone. Their spiritual activities and "performance" flow naturally, and they may not even be aware of the impact they're having on the world around them.

Rapid Spiritual Growth Marks Spiritual Maturity

Movement 3 is the time when spiritual growth is most rapid, which may seem counterintuitive. We might expect people to report that they are growing rapidly earlier in their spiritual journey, when they first become familiar with the power of prayer and Scripture. However, the growth of those in Movement 3 appears to be the most fruitful and accelerated (chart 3-11). More Christ-Centered people are likely to report a rapid pace of spiritual growth than those in any other segment, and the incline from Close to Christ to Christ-Centered (Movement 3) is steep, which means it's significant.

This rapid growth experience in Movement 3 tracks again with the analogy of a student's college experience. It is in college that people move beyond the basic high school curriculum to higher levels of critical thinking and increased diversity of academic and personal challenges. They also focus increasing attention on their chosen field of study. Likewise, Christ-Centered people seek out higher levels of growth and a greater diversity of spiritual experiences, and they also exhibit a laserlike focus on their faith. These characteristics create an environment in which accelerated growth is a logical outcome.

Those in the Christ-Centered Segment Are Most Likely to Say They Are in a Season of Rapid Spiritual Growth

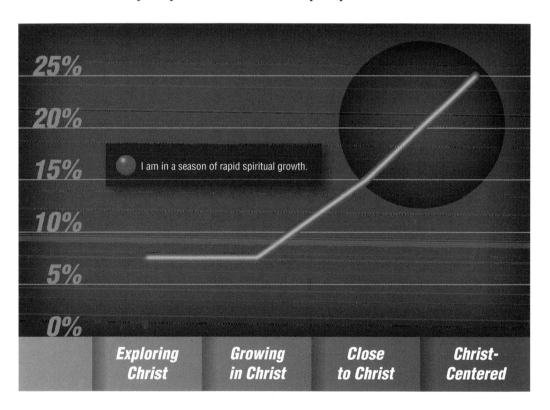

Chart 3-11: The Christ-Centered segment is much more likely than any other segment to say "I am in a season of rapid spiritual growth."

Movement 3 Is a Time of Spiritual Generosity

Movement 3 is a time when people open their hearts fully to Christ's call on their lives. We see evidence of this in the escalation of their "very strongly agree" responses to four spiritual attitude statements (chart 3-12).

"Giving away my life" is the catalytic attitude that demonstrates the greatest acceleration for those moving from the Close to Christ segment to the Christ-Centered segment. This means increasing

Attitudes about Giving Away My Time, My Money, My Faith and My Life Increase Dramatically in the Advanced Segments of Spiritual Growth

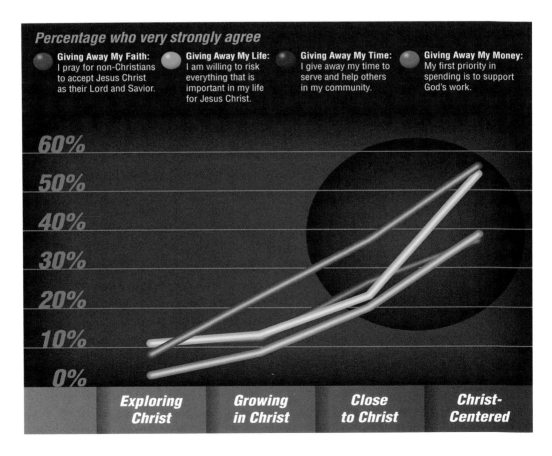

Chart 3-12: The percentage of people who "very strongly agree" with spiritual attitude statements about surrendering the most important aspects of life to God rises significantly between the Close to Christ and Christ-Centered segments. This demonstrates a spiritual heart shift from a self-centered identity to an identity defined by a relationship with Christ.

numbers of people in Movement 3 "very strongly agree" that "I am willing to risk everything that is important in my life for Jesus Christ."

This increased willingness to turn over "everything that is important" to Christ—from finances, to time, to one's life—is not an empty promise. Spiritual behavior patterns rise in response as people align their actions with their hearts. The rapid spiritual growth and increasing attitudes of surrender that characterize Movement 3 appear to be fed by this increasing spiritual activity (chart 3-13).

Spiritual behavior patterns rise in response as people align their actions with their hearts.

The Most Advanced Segments Have the Highest Levels of Serving, Evangelism and Tithing

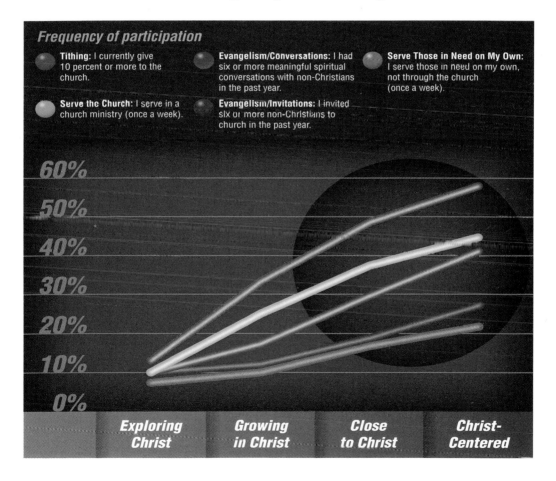

Frequency of participation

- **Tithing:** I currently give 10 percent or more to the church.
- **Serve the Church:** I serve in a church ministry (once a week).
- **Evangelism/Conversations:** I had six or more meaningful spiritual conversations with non-Christians in the past year.
- **Evangelism/Invitations:** I invited six or more non-Christians to church in the past year.
- **Serve Those in Need on My Own:** I serve those in need on my own, not through the church (once a week).

60%
50%
40%
30%
20%
10%
0%

Exploring Christ | Growing in Christ | Close to Christ | Christ-Centered

Chart 3-13: The frequency of tithing, serving and evangelism rises to its highest levels in the Close to Christ and Christ-Centered segments (circled), illustrating the outpouring of spiritual behavior associated with increasing spiritual maturity.

In Movement 3, spiritual growth is stoked internally.

We believe activities such as serving and evangelism are not simply triggered by increasing faith, but that the activities themselves actually catalyze spiritual growth. If you'll indulge one more reference to the college experience, these activities are similar to internships when students have their first opportunity to apply academic knowledge and training to a real-life situation. Their knowledge and excitement about their chosen field grows by using their academic gifts on the job in an active learning environment.

Serving and evangelism are those kinds of active learning experiences for the Christ-Centered people. We believe such experiences are not simply outputs from a devoted faith, but catalytic growth events themselves. This belief is based on the high degree of correlation we see between rapid growth, attitudes of surrender and increasing spiritual activities. In Movement 3, spiritual growth is nourished by spiritual outreach activities, and vice versa; each one inspires and promotes the other.

The Top Five Spiritual Catalysts for Movement 3

In Movement 3, spiritual growth is stoked internally. We say this because the top four catalysts are beliefs or attitudes—convictions of the mind and heart—that drive an outpouring of faith-based surrender and action (chart 3-14).

Does the fact that none of the spiritual activities like evangelism or serving show up in the top five catalysts conflict with our earlier observations about the power of these experiences to trigger growth?

No. If we expanded the top five catalysts to a top-ten list, those activities would be right on the heels of the beliefs and attitudes we see here. What chart 3-14 does is reinforce the central conclusion of all our research—which is that spiritual growth is not about increasing activities; it is about growing an increasingly intimate relationship with Christ. The four beliefs and attitudes at the top of the list

Movement 3:
From Close to Christ to Christ-Centered

The Top Five Catalysts Influencing Movement 3*

1. **Giving Away My Life** (Spiritual Belief / Attitude)

2. **Christ Is First** (Spiritual Belief / Attitude)

3. **Identity in Christ** (Spiritual Belief / Attitude)

4. **Authority of the Bible** (Spiritual Belief / Attitude)

5. **Reflection on Scripture** (Spiritual Practice)

* Listed in order of importance. See appendix 2, "Research Approach and Methodology" (page 144), for a more detailed explanation of the statistical approach used for analysis.

Chart 3-14: The top five spiritual catalysts out of the more than fifty factors evaluated are listed in order of importance for Movement 3. These five factors represent the combination of catalysts that are most predictive of movement from Close to Christ to Christ-Centered.

underscore that the relationship with Christ is what's important, not the activities.

The first attitude statement, "giving away my life," is a vanilla factor; its predictability is more than twice the predictability of the other four factors. This means that agreement with the statement "I am willing to surrender everything that is important in my life to Jesus Christ" is the most powerful predictor of a Christ-Centered heart.

The "Christ is first" attitude ("I desire Jesus to be first in my life") is a strong second influence—similar to chocolate on the ice cream flavor scale—ranking higher than the other three by a solid margin.

If our observations about the correlation between these very strong spiritual attitudes and increased spiritual activities (evangelism, serving) are correct, this is incredibly good news and signals an enormous opportunity for the church. Why?

Let's go back to the Michael Jordan example. When the game was on the line and the Bulls saw that Michael was in the zone—hitting

Spiritual growth is not about increasing activities; it is about growing an increasingly intimate relationship with Christ.

baskets at will and playing near-perfect defense—they knew which strategy to follow.

Give Michael the ball.

In essence, that's the same strategy the church needs to follow with those in Movement 3. These spiritually fired-up people need very little from the church to help them grow—very little, at least, in terms of new Bible study programs or worship events. What they need is for the church to give them "the ball."

They need the church to engage them as full partners in a divine pact to carry out Christ's Great Commission.

Those in Movement 3 need high-level encouragement and coaching that calls out the spiritual behaviors so aligned with their hearts. They need opportunities to stretch their serving and evangelistic experiences beyond the typical menu of church ministry options. They need the church to engage them as full partners in a divine pact to carry out Christ's Great Commission. In the spirit of the Michael Jordan story, Christ-Centered people are the ball game for the kingdom. Inspiring, coaching, encouraging and equipping these people with opportunities to serve the lost and the underresourced should be our highest priority.

On hearing these findings about Movement 3, the pastor of a church who participated in the early phases of our research made an observation that's right on target: "I spend 80 percent of my time and resources on people who are in the early stages of growth," he said. "What you're telling me is that if I took some of that 80 percent and spent it on these Christ-Centered people, they would partner with me and help me grow all those people who are just beginning their spiritual journeys." Absolutely right.

The Christ-Centered people are the ball game. This was the biggest story to come out of our initial research in 2004 when the only church surveyed was Willow Creek. This was also the most significant finding when we expanded our research to seven churches in early 2007. To date, we've surveyed over 200 churches, and the headline is the same—the Christ-Centered people offer the greatest high-impact opportunity for the church and the kingdom.

SPIRITUAL GROWTH— CAN WE KEEP IT SIMPLE?

Spiritual growth is not linear or predictable (chart 3-15). It is a complex process as unique as each individual, and it progresses at a pace determined by each person's circumstances and the activity of the Holy Spirit. This observation, while true, makes spiritual growth feel very complicated—difficult to understand, hard to resource and support, impossible to measure. The encouragement from our latest research is that, while spiritual growth is complex, there appears to be a simplicity in its general progression that may help us to think about it differently, to resource it better and to encourage it more productively.

It is a complex process as unique as each individual.

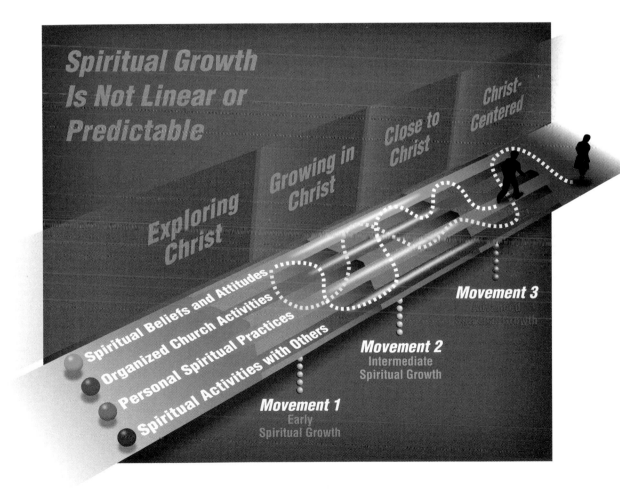

Chart 3-15: Each individual follows a unique spiritual growth pathway.

Our findings suggest that no matter where someone is on the spiritual continuum, their journey is influenced in some way by four categories of spiritual catalysts: spiritual beliefs and attitudes, church activities, personal spiritual practices and spiritual activities with others.

Our findings also suggest that these spiritual catalysts are generally progressive and are correlated with three spiritual movements.

Movement 1

Movement 1 is the early movement of spiritual growth, and it's all about Christian fundamentals. Building a firm foundation of spiritual beliefs and attitudes is particularly important. The impact of church activities on spiritual growth is most significant in this movement.

Movement 2

Movement 2 is the intermediate movement of spiritual growth; it hinges on developing a routine of personal spiritual practices that feed a growing intimacy with Christ.

Movement 3

Movement 3 is the advanced movement of spiritual growth, made up of "in the zone" Christ-Centered followers who fully surrender their hearts and pour out their love for Jesus through spiritual outreach activities.

It is possible to think of spiritual growth in less complicated terms.

In spite of the complexity and emotional context of the spiritual experience, perhaps the most important takeaway from this chapter is that it is possible to think of spiritual growth in less complicated terms. Because, while each person's spiritual path is distinct, when we pool together thousands of individual surveys describing spiritual experiences, a general pattern emerges that transcends individual results.

While we acknowledge that the process of spiritual growth is unique for each person and also acknowledge that there will always be an enormous unexplained dimension to spirituality, the simplicity of these three spiritual movements does give us something we can act on—with a high level of confidence that our decisions will make a difference in the lives of those we serve.

IN CHAPTER 2, WE INTRODUCED the three spiritual movements using the metaphor of a spiritual symphony (pages 47–48). But most symphonies have four movements, not three. Likewise, the spiritual continuum actually has a fourth movement as well. We call it the "missing movement" (chart 3-16).

This missing movement precedes Movement 1. Because our research to date has focused on people who attend church, we have little data on the people who don't attend church—those whom we describe as "Far from God." So we don't have anything beyond speculation about what predicts movement from being Far from God to Exploring Christ.

While we plan to eventually do more research on the Far from God segment, we do have some initial hypotheses about their greatest

obstacles to faith (chart 3-17, page 80). Based on observations from studying the Exploring Christ segment, we believe these are the five most critical catalysts that will inspire spiritual growth in those who are Far from God.

continued on next page

Chart 3-16: A missing spiritual movement emerges when those who are Far from God are included on the spiritual continuum.

The (Missing) Movement (cont.)

Our hypothesis is that the biggest spiritual stumbling block for this group is belief in the Trinity ("I believe the God of the Bible is the one true God—Father, Son and Holy Spirit"). We see evidence that this obstacle might be overcome by the influence of spiritual friends, the experience of answered prayer, hearing messages in weekend services and exposure to Scripture.

This missing movement is a "sweet spot" in which the church can join forces with Christ-Centered people to advance the message of faith to those least likely to be tuned in. ✦

The Missing Movement:
Far from God to Exploring Christ

Moving from Being Far from God to Exploring Christ	
Spiritual Beliefs and Attitudes	The Trinity
Church Activities	Weekend Services
Personal Spiritual Practices	Prayer to Seek Guidance (*rare to occasional*) Reflection on Scripture (*never to rarely*)
Spiritual Activities with Others	Spiritual Friendships

Chart 3-17: Based on findings from the Exploring Christ segment, these five spiritual catalysts may be the most important factors likely to inspire those who are Far from God to consider Christianity.

CALLY PARKINSON

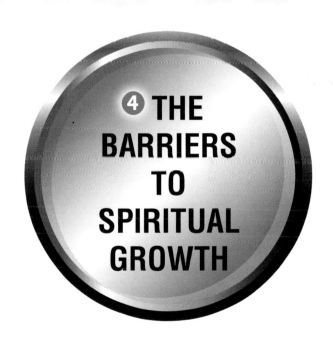

④ THE BARRIERS TO SPIRITUAL GROWTH

TWO STUMBLING BLOCKS TO SPIRITUAL PROGRESS

barriers

THE SPIRITUAL JOURNEY is not without its frustrations. Many churchgoers say they are derailed from their relationship with God or the church. How does this happen? What are the barriers that get in the way of spiritual growth? And what can we do about them?

4

THE BARRIERS TO SPIRITUAL GROWTH

In October 1947, Chuck Yeager became the first person to break the sound barrier, flying in excess of 770 mph at an altitude of 45,000 feet. This feat was achieved due to aircraft design improvements that addressed the aerodynamic issues that caused planes to malfunction and even crash when they approached the speed of sound. Modern day aircraft routinely transition through the sound barrier with minimal disturbance. However, today's smooth ride depends on having both the right equipment and a well-trained pilot.

Spiritual growth faces its own version of the sound barrier. In fact, our research discovered two critical barriers that cause disruptive shocks and severe turbulence along the spiritual journey. Virtually everyone we surveyed acknowledged experiencing one of these barriers at some point in their spiritual development. Like the barrier-breaking success of high-speed flight, we found that successfully navigating beyond these barriers depends largely on how well people are spiritually equipped, coached and trained.

The first barrier involves an experience not unfamiliar to many Christ-followers—the barrier of being stalled.

Our research discovered two critical barriers that cause disruptive shocks and severe turbulence along the spiritual journey.

BARRIER 1:
"I HAVE STALLED SPIRITUALLY"

"I want to quit!"

These words are familiar to most parents. When our children face homework that is too hard or a coach who is too demanding, they sometimes feel like giving up. In this case, my twelve-year-old daughter's frustration with her piano lessons had reached a boiling point. "I want to quit!" she declared after a particularly difficult lesson.

Being stalled means being stuck, mired, hindered or slowed down.

What's a parent to do? Up to this point, she loved playing the piano, but now it was a source of anxiety and created friction between her and her teacher. She was angry at the piano, angry at her teacher, but most of all, angry and disappointed in herself. In effect, she was stalled, and it seemed easier to quit than to figure out how to become unstalled.

Being stalled means being stuck, mired, hindered or slowed down. We all know what a frustrating feeling this is. Just think of the last time you tried to start your car and all you heard was the grinding of the ignition because the engine failed to turn over. You were stalled and couldn't get where you were going, which was likely pretty aggravating.

Those who are spiritually stalled feel a similar frustration. A disruption in spiritual momentum puts them in a tough spot, and now they face some unexpected and/or unpleasant decisions about what they need to do to get back on track. Unfortunately, unlike the stalled car—where you eventually have to do something to get where you're going—spiritually stalled people can decide to quit altogether and avoid the difficult decisions necessary to reengage their journey toward Christ. The higher the level of frustration, the more likely it is that they'll quit.

More than one in five (22 percent) of those surveyed (80,000 people from more than 200 congregations) describe their current spiritual growth as "stalled." They had the option to select three other statements to describe their spiritual growth, including "I'm in a state of rapid spiritual growth" or "I'm in a state of reasonable spiritual growth" or "I'm content with my spiritual growth." But they chose "I have stalled spiritually."

Spiritually stalled people can decide to quit altogether.

Those who are stalled exist in all segments across the spiritual continuum, but most of them fall within the first two segments of spiritual growth (chart 4-1).

People Who Say "I Have Stalled Spiritually" Fall Mostly in the Earlier Segments of Spiritual Growth

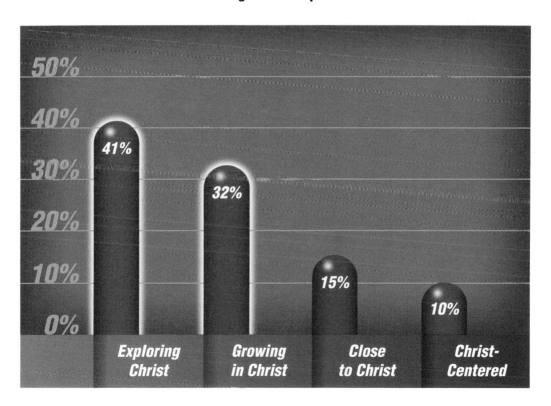

Chart 4-1: The highest percentages of people who say "I have stalled spiritually" fall in the Exploring Christ and Growing in Christ segments (highlighted). This means that becoming stalled spiritually is much more likely to occur in Movement 1.

Obstacles occur primarily at the beginning of the journey.

This suggests that the obstacles that cause people to stall spiritually occur primarily at the beginning of the journey. These obstacles don't appear to be related to foundational beliefs and attitudes. Agreement with core Christian beliefs like the Trinity and salvation by grace is similar for those who are stalled and not stalled. However, they express lower levels of agreement with beliefs about a personal God and the authority of the Bible (chart 4-2).

The Core Christian Beliefs of Those Who Are Stalled Are Similar to Those Who Are Not Stalled

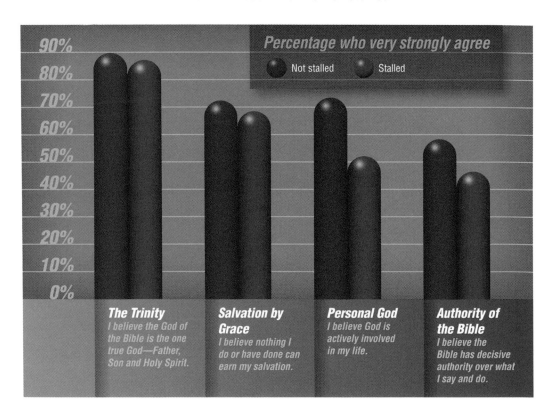

Chart 4-2: Comparing the "very strongly agree" responses to four core Christian beliefs, those who are stalled are very similar to those who are not stalled in terms of their belief in the Trinity and salvation by grace. Their lower responses regarding their belief in a personal God and belief in the authority of the Bible are more likely due to their general lack of maturity as a Christian than their status of being stalled.

This pattern of agreement with beliefs makes sense when you recall that the stalled people come primarily from Movement 1. The first two beliefs are highly influential in Movement 1, while the second two beliefs tend to be more influential as people advance through Movements 2 and 3 (chart 2-4, page 32). So it's logical that the stalled group would believe as strongly in the Trinity and salvation by grace as the unstalled group, but less strongly in the truth of a personal God and

The stalled people come primarily from Movement 1.

Those Who Are Stalled Report More Significant Barriers Than Those Who Are Not Stalled

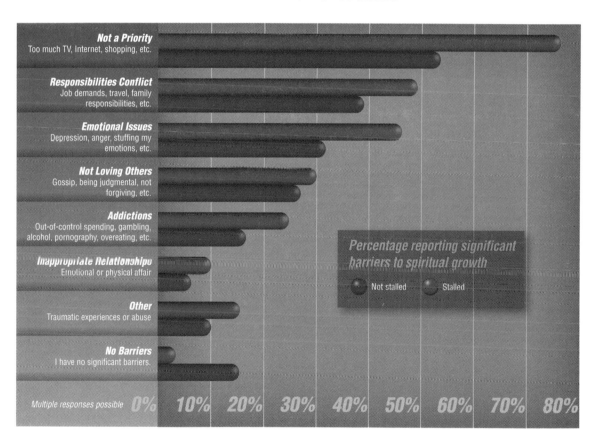

Chart 4-3: Those who are stalled report far more personal barriers to growth as well as a very high response to spiritual growth being "not a priority." This suggests that the combination of a low-priority spiritual life and personal issues triggers being stalled.

Emotional problems, addictions and inappropriate relationships are barriers to their growth.

the authority of the Bible. This is due more to their lower level of spiritual development (being in Movement 1) rather than their status of being stalled.

So what causes people who believe strongly in God and salvation by grace to stall out spiritually? We find that those who are stalled are more likely than others to report "significant barriers" (chart 4-3, page 87). They report that personal issues like emotional problems, addictions and inappropriate relationships are barriers to their growth, causing disruption and turbulence in their spiritual progress. But the most significant barrier by far is that they are "not making spiritual growth a high priority."

Those Who Are Stalled Report Much Lower Levels of Personal Spiritual Practices Than Those Who Are Not Stalled

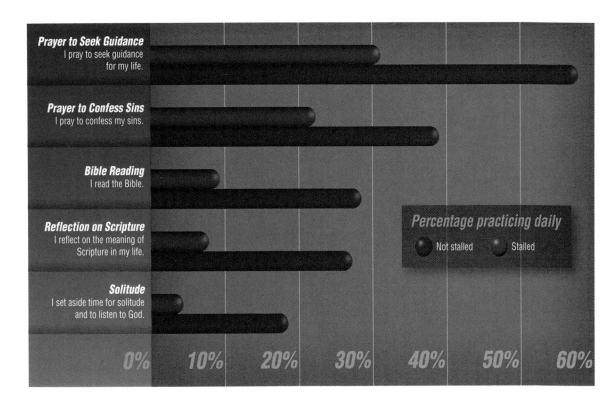

Chart 4-4: Those who are stalled report very low engagement levels with personal spiritual practices. This is consistent with their high responses to spiritual growth being "not a priority."

The fact that those who are stalled don't make spiritual growth a priority is reinforced by our next finding—that those who are stalled report markedly lower levels of personal spiritual practices than those who are not stalled (chart 4-4). These low investments of time in personal spiritual development appear to be a direct reflection of the stalled group's admission that "not making spiritual growth a priority" is a significant barrier for them. The dramatically low percentages of daily Bible reading and reflection on Scripture (each one less than 10 percent) are a critical concern given the Bible's significant influence on spiritual growth (chart 2-7, page 42).

"Not making spiritual growth a priority" is a significant barrier.

These findings about the stalled group are consistent with our previous research. Based on our earlier work, we suggested that those who are stalled might be spiritually unprepared to face life's challenges because their personal relationship with Christ is not anchored in a consistent rhythm of spiritual practices. When the storms of life come along, it's possible that the roots of their faith are too shallow, and their spiritual journey stalls from frustration and doubts about God's faithfulness (Matthew 13:6). Having shallow spiritual roots withers faith, and that's what we see in the stalled segment.

> *We now have findings that provide insight on what it takes to get people unstalled.*

We asked everyone taking our most recent survey if there was ever a time in their spiritual journey when they were stalled. Virtually every respondent said yes. We then asked what happened to get them unstalled. The overwhelming majority said they became unstalled by reengaging in personal spiritual practices (chart 4-5, page 90).

While we don't know what triggered the decisions to reengage, we do know that spiritual practices were responsible for getting people back on track with their spiritual growth. Why this is true might be explained by revisiting the story of my daughter's piano lesson meltdown.

She was adamant that her piano-playing days were over. To be honest, I didn't care if she continued with the lessons or not; I just didn't want her to give up out of feelings of frustration and failure. In one of my more brilliant parenting moves, I agreed on the spot that she could quit—on one condition. I asked her to spend twenty minutes every day during the next week practicing piano. If she did that and still walked out of her next lesson convinced she wanted to quit, I would support her decision.

People "Unstall" by Reengaging in Spiritual Practices

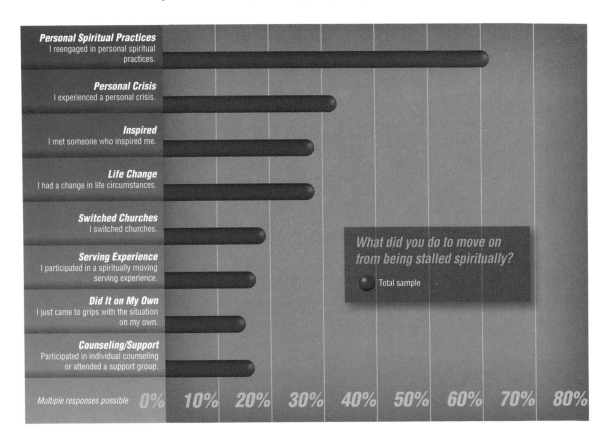

Chart 4-5: Virtually everyone surveyed reported a stalled experience in their spiritual journey. When asked how they were able to "unstall," the most common answer by far was to reengage in spiritual practices. Only half as many marked the second highest response, "I experienced a personal crisis."

She agreed. And she didn't quit. In fact, she continued taking piano until she went to college six years later. There were a few more bumps of frustration along the way, but once she buckled down and reengaged in her discipline of daily practice, she got herself back on track. Why did this work? Because she loved the music. She loved playing the piano and the music it created. Playing the piano tapped into a passion that was reengaged by a renewed discipline of daily practice.

This same dynamic may explain the power personal spiritual practices have to catalyze growth in a spiritually stalled heart. Reengaging in personal spiritual practices rekindles our love for Christ and our belief in his love for us. It is our belief in that love and God's faithfulness that keeps us strong in the face of life's burdens and pressures.

Life's curveballs can be tough and they can happen at any point along the spiritual continuum. These findings about the stalled group are a testimony to the importance of building a consistent rhythm of spiritual practices into our lives. We are all vulnerable to stalling. Personal spiritual practices reinforce our faith by providing constant reminders of God's presence in our lives, which is the greatest insurance of all for keeping us spiritually unstalled.

Spiritual practices were responsible for getting people back on track.

BARRIER 2:
"I AM DISSATISFIED"

Think back to your decision about where to go for college, seminary or any kind of ongoing education or training. You probably chose an institution based on many factors—cost, location, size, campus environment, expertise in your chosen field, reputation, etc. These factors served as a filter for your decision to enroll in a specific institution for the purpose of academic growth and professional/personal development.

That decision eventually became a real experience. From the first day of sizing up your peers and finding your classrooms, you judged your satisfaction with your experience against the expectations established by the factors that informed your original decision. So if your choice

*Seventeen
percent
express some
level of
dissatisfaction
with their
church.*

was based on the institution's expertise in your chosen field, but your professors were uninspiring and dull, you probably weren't very happy.

That's what satisfaction and dissatisfaction are all about. They are personal judgments about whether or not an experience exceeds, meets or misses the mark of expectations.

What shapes expectations for our church experience? This is a critical question because the research shows a relatively high percentage of people—17 percent—express some level of dissatisfaction with their church. This dissatisfaction is not focused on tangential issues like poor parking, loud music or uncomfortable seats. They are specifi-

Dissatisfied People Are Present in All Segments

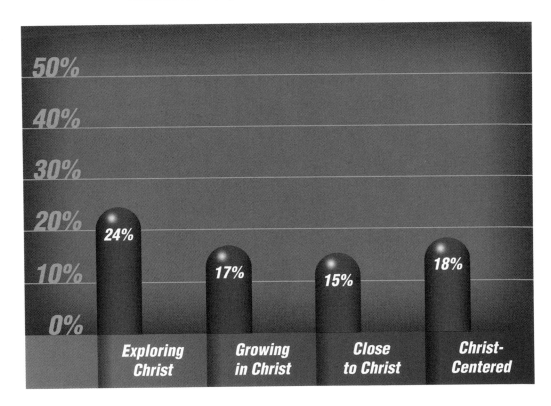

Chart 4-6: The people who are dissatisfied with their church's role in their spiritual growth are distributed fairly evenly across the four spiritual segments. In total, 17 percent of those surveyed expressed some level of dissatisfaction with their church.

92

cally dissatisfied with "how the church helps me grow spiritually," which means they see the church as an obstacle, not an aid, to their spiritual development.

These dissatisfied people exist in all segments of the spiritual continuum, so the church is not meeting the expectations of the dissatisfied group across all spiritual movements, largely in equal measure (chart 4-6).

As a barrier to spiritual growth, dissatisfaction differs somewhat from being stalled. Spiritual growth is truly blocked for people who are stalled, which isn't necessarily the case for the dissatisfied. Our findings show that the patterns of spiritual beliefs, attitudes and practices for the dissatisfied are comparable to those of similar spiritual maturity who are not dissatisfied with the role of the church in their spiritual development. So dissatisfaction is not a barrier that blocks spiritual growth. Instead, it could be that dissatisfaction compromises and frustrates the potential for spiritual development much like a poor teacher compromises learning. You can learn a subject in spite of a poor teacher by reading an academic text, but frustration with the teaching may put a lid on your enjoyment of the subject, as well as your grasp of the material. Likewise, the disappointment dissatisfied people experience with the church limits their ability to fully engage with the church's spiritual instruction and encouragement. Ultimately, this disappointment causes many of them to leave their church. Both dissatisfaction and being stalled are barriers to growth but the outcomes differ: the stalled quit the spiritual journey; the dissatisfied quit the church.

Dissatisfaction compromises and frustrates the potential for spiritual development.

If we can figure out the factors that are most influential to setting the expectations people have for church, we can identify what factors are most influential to satisfaction or dissatisfaction. Importantly, the factor that's most influential to satisfaction will tend to be the same factor that's most influential to dissatisfaction. In other words, the key to understanding the source of dissatisfaction is to understand which factor is most important to someone when they judge the quality of their experience. Which factor is most significant to setting expectations for what the experience of church is going to be like?

We can identify the cause of dissatisfaction with the church by look-ing at the church activities that are most highly correlated with people's satisfaction with the church's role in helping them grow spir-itually. By a wide margin, the weekend service is the church activity most highly correlated with church satisfaction. In fact, the weekend service is more significant to people's satisfaction with the church by a factor of four compared to all other church activities. Using the analogy of choosing a college, this would be similar to selecting a school because of its expertise in your chosen field *in spite of* other negative factors, such as the cost of the school being well beyond your budget, the campus environment being unappealing and the distance from home being greater than you wanted. How well that school delivers against your expectation of its expertise in your chosen field is crucial to how satisfied you are with your school experience because that factor is head and shoulders above all others in its importance to you.

The weekend service is the church activity most highly correlated with church satisfaction.

Based on our research, the weekend service is that kind of over-the-top factor in its importance to people's satisfaction with how the church helps them grow spiritually. We can conclude, then, that if the weekend service is producing the most satisfaction with the church, it's also the source of the most dissatisfaction.

Sources of Dissatisfaction

What do dissatisfied people want from the weekend service? Chart 4-7 compares how the dissatisfied group rates the importance of, and their satisfaction with, ten elements associated with the weekend service experience.

The first column on the chart ranks the percentage of the dissatisfied group who marked each element as "critically" or "very important." This is analogous to our observations about setting expectations. The factors rated as most important are the ones most influential in shaping the dissatisfied group's expectations for the weekend service.

Sources of Dissatisfaction with Weekend Services
(Dissatisfied Group Only)

Ten Elements of Weekend Services	Importance [1]	Satisfaction [2]	THE GAP [3]
Incorporates relevant Bible teaching to help me with everyday life	87%	32%	55%
Is challenging or thought provoking	84%	30%	54%
Incorporates frequent use of Scripture	81%	41%	41%
Provides in-depth study of the Bible	72%	19%	53%
Incorporates worship music and congregational singing effectively	68%	50%	18%
Provide next steps—things I can do in response	60%	20%	40%
Provides an opportunity for reflection and guided prayer	55%	22%	33%
Incorporates stories and testimonies of real people	45%	37%	8%
Makes tools available (print, Internet) so I can process the message during the week	38%	35%	3%
Incorporates creative elements, like live drama, dance or video	27%	50%	-23% *

[1] Percentage of those who rated the statement as "critically" or "very important" [2] Percentage who said they were "extremely" or "very satisfied" [3] Importance minus satisfaction

* This negative gap means that satisfaction is higher than importance.

Chart 4-7: Those who are dissatisfied with the church's role in their spiritual growth rated ten elements related to weekend services on importance and satisfaction. Satisfaction was subtracted from importance to determine the biggest gaps, indicating areas of opportunity for church strategy.

The second column shows the percentage who were "extremely" or "very satisfied" with how they experienced these elements at their church's weekend service. In the third column, we subtract satisfaction from importance so we can better understand where the church is missing the mark by the widest margin according to our dissatisfied people. Here are two important insights from this analysis.

Three weekend service elements are most important. Over 80 percent of the dissatisfied group rated the following three elements as "critically" or "very important" to their weekend service experience:

- *"Relevant Bible teaching to help me with everyday life"*

- *"Is challenging or thought provoking"*

- *"Incorporates frequent use of Scripture"*

These factors ranked much higher than the others, so it would appear that they set the tone for the dissatisfied group's expectations. Importantly, everyone—regardless of satisfaction level—ranked these same three elements of weekend services as most important. This means that these three elements are most critical to shaping the expectations for everyone, not just the dissatisfied group.

Three weekend service elements show significant gaps between the importance and satisfaction. Based on responses from the dissatisfied group only (chart 4-7, page 95), there are significant gaps between importance and satisfaction for three weekend service elements:

- *"Relevant Bible teaching to help me with everyday life"*

- *"Is challenging or thought provoking"*

- *"Provides in-depth study of the Bible"*

These are the biggest sources of discontent for the dissatisfied group and potentially the most significant opportunity to reduce dissatisfaction with the church. Importantly, these factors are also the elements with the biggest gaps between importance and satisfaction for those who are satisfied with the church's role in their spiritual growth. Bringing more church resources to bear against these three elements would address the gaps expressed by virtually everyone— regardless of their level of satisfaction or dissatisfaction.

But let's be clear.

The gaps of more than 50 percent for the dissatisfied people (chart 4-7, page 95) are much higher than the gaps expressed by those who are satisfied with the church. People who are happy with the church's role in their spiritual growth naturally express high satisfaction with the most important church activity—weekend services. While these three elements are the most significant unmet expectations for all people, the gaps between importance and satisfaction for those who are satisfied with the church's role in their spiritual growth are around 10 to 12 percent compared with the more than 50 percent gaps for those who are dissatisfied.

These three gaps reflect areas of general weakness for the church.

The most important insight from this analysis is that these three gaps reflect areas of general weakness for the church and this weakness is not exclusive to those who express dissatisfaction. In other words, addressing the three unmet expectations expressed by the dissatisfied for weekend services would resonate with all people, regardless of their satisfaction with the church and no matter where they are on their spiritual journey.

Understanding the Dissatisfied

Based on these observations about sources of dissatisfaction plus additional findings from our analysis of this segment, we offer the following five reasons why we believe the church should view the dissatisfied group as a high-value, high-impact opportunity.

They shine a light where we need to look. The dissatisfied put a spotlight on the primary sources of discontent within the church, but their views on the church's weaknesses are shared—to some extent—by everyone. The fact that both the dissatisfied and the satisfied agree on the importance of the same weekend service elements as well as the same three unmet expectations is an indication that the dissatisfied group can point the way to improvements that will advance everyone's spiritual growth. This suggests that we should pay attention to those complaining e-mails when we see consistent patterns in the source of the grumbling; it appears the dissatisfied may be a bellwether for the entire congregation's view of needed change in the church.

They are misunderstood. When I think about the dissatisfied people, the image that comes to mind is a picture of Grumpy, one of Snow White's seven dwarfs. I imagine the dissatisfied group as a crowd of Grumpys—scowling, cranky, complaining and generally unappreciative human beings.

Those who are dissatisfied are not chronically negative people.

But our analysis shows this isn't an accurate image. Those who are dissatisfied are not chronically negative people. In fact, most of them demonstrate a fired-up faith and a servant's heart. Also, their demographics are consistent with those of the total sample; they aren't older or younger than the rest of the church population. And they're not habitual church hoppers; on average, their church tenure exceeds seven years.

These are faithful people who express unmet expectations for the church. Everything in our data says that we should listen to them.

They are not entrenched. "Like the poor, they'll always be with us," said one pastor in describing the dissatisfied group. But according to our data, that's not true. The dissatisfied people are not entrenched in their frustration with the church. Evidence for this is the wide range of dissatisfied percentages in the more than 200 churches we surveyed. The highest dissatisfied percentage for a single church congregation is 42 percent; the lowest dissatisfaction percentage is 6 percent. While no church has zero dissatisfaction, a number of churches are in the single digits.

This range of high to low dissatisfaction percentages, added to the number of churches at the low end of the range, suggests that a church can influence and shift the levels of dissatisfaction within its congregation. And the good news is that it appears dissatisfaction can be reduced by meeting the needs expressed by the entire congregation. It's like the old saying, "A rising tide lifts all boats."

They aren't leaving. We asked people if they were "definitely" or "probably staying at the church," "definitely" or "probably leaving the church" or "unsure if I'm staying or leaving." While 41 percent of the dissatisfied said they were unsure or probably/definitely leaving, the other 59 percent plan to stay at the church. More importantly, most—over two-thirds—of the 41 percent say they are unsure, so they aren't on their way out the door—yet. We still have a chance to reclaim these people as advocates, not detractors, of the church.

These people are deeply committed to Jesus Christ but struggle with the church.

Many are devoted Christ-followers. Over half of the dissatisfied come from the most advanced movement of spiritual growth, which means they are among our best evangelists, donors and volunteers. These people are deeply committed to Jesus Christ but struggle with the church. All of our research points to the potential impact of passionate Christ-followers. If we can overcome this barrier of church dissatisfaction, we will prevent the loss of these people from the church. More importantly, we could convert these Christ-Centered church critics into fully engaged church partners, advancing kingdom work instead of kingdom discontent.

The Dissatisfied-Stalled Overlap

Dissatisfaction can turn into a magnet for greater dissatisfaction. A few disappointments can cloud our vision and create anticipation that more setbacks are on the way. "The sky is falling" is not an uncommon feeling for people caught in this kind of discouraging cycle of real and perceived letdowns.

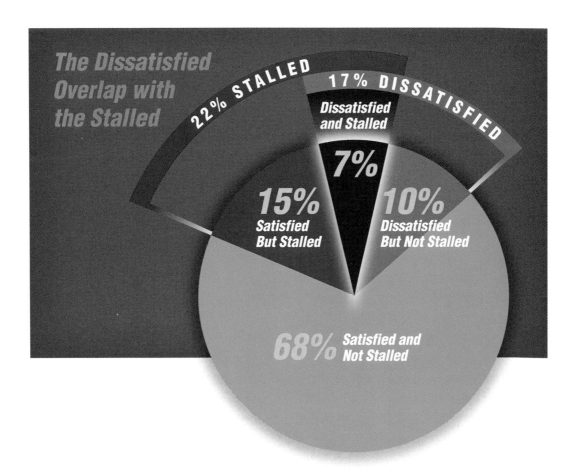

Chart 4-8: There is an overlap between the 17 percent dissatisfied people and the 22 percent who are stalled. Seven percent of the total sample are both stalled and dissatisfied. Adding together the highlighted sections of the stalled and/or dissatisfied shows that 32 percent (the sum of 15, 7 and 10 percent) of the total sample fall into these two groups.

THE BARRIERS TO SPIRITUAL GROWTH

It's not surprising that our two most disillusioned spiritual segments share common characteristics and, to some extent, feed off of each other. If someone is stalled and unhappy with their spiritual life, it's logical that they might blame the church for that situation. Likewise, because the church is so central to the early stages of spiritual growth, it makes sense that dissatisfaction with the church could cause someone to stall out spiritually. In fact, 7 percent of those surveyed (chart 4-8) fall into an overlapping category of people who are both unhappy with their church (dissatisfied) and unhappy with their own spiritual growth (stalled).

Our two most disillusioned spiritual segments share common characteristics.

There is good news.

The good news is that 68 percent of all those surveyed are both satisfied and not stalled. They are growing spiritually and they're happy with the role the church plays in their spiritual growth. In the 200 churches surveyed, this number ranged from a high of 84 percent to a low of 48 percent—a wide span that demonstrates the enormous impact different church strategies and formats have on people's spiritual lives.

Another piece of good news is that 15 percent are satisfied with the church's role in their spiritual growth despite the fact that they are stalled. This group would likely welcome strategies from the church designed to help them become unstalled.

There is also bad news.

The bad news is that when we look at the net number of stalled and dissatisfied people (adding together the highlighted sections of the stalled and/or dissatisfied), we see that almost one-third of those surveyed (32 percent) fall into these struggling, unhappy groups. Although 32 percent is discouraging, we do see wide variation in these percentages among the churches surveyed. This means that one of the greatest contributions from this research work is still in front of us— and that is to create a process that enables us to learn from each other. If we could look beneath the hood of the churches with the lowest percentages of these two negatively charged segments, we would hope to discover the strategies and programs that seem most effective at addressing the needs of the stalled and dissatisfied. If we can spread the word about those strategies and programs, the gains in spiritual energy and productivity could be remarkable.

In the meantime, we can begin to act on what we know now. We know the stalled group's greatest opportunity and obstacle is the challenge to reengage in personal spiritual practices. We know that at the heart of the dissatisfied group's discontent is a perceived lack of relevant biblical teaching, challenge and use of Scripture in weekend services.

It is possible—knowing no more than we know now—to take early steps to help those who are stalled and dissatisfied.

These are barriers we can overcome.

It is possible—knowing no more than we know now—to take early steps to help those who are stalled and dissatisfied navigate the disruptive shocks and turbulence that challenge their spiritual journeys. These are barriers we can overcome; it just requires spiritual equipping, encouragement, coaching and training. Then the stalled will reengage with their passion for Christ, and the dissatisfied will reengage with their passion for the church. And a growing body of Christ-followers will be back on the path to living out fully committed, Christ-Centered lives.

CALLY PARKINSON

FOLLOW ME

⑤ TWO BREAKTHROUGH DISCOVERIES

THE TOP TWO FINDINGS FROM OUR SURVEY OF OVER 200 CHURCHES

discoveries

WE SEARCHED THROUGH four years of research on spiritual growth to identify two breakthrough findings with far-reaching implications for the church. Both discoveries shed light on what we can do right now to have the greatest impact on spiritual growth.

⑤

TWO BREAKTHROUGH DISCOVERIES

The REVEAL team recently gathered together to reflect on everything our research has discovered so far. We put away the data and the charts and turned off the computers. Then we debated and discussed our primary findings, searching our hearts and minds for what we felt were the biggest breakthrough discoveries from our four years of research. We used the word *breakthrough* intentionally because a breakthrough goes well beyond interesting findings and incremental impact. A breakthrough is a new discovery with dramatic and far-reaching implications. That was the focus of several hours of conversation. We wanted to identify what we felt were truly far-reaching discoveries—the ones with the most dramatic potential for kingdom impact. Here is what we came up with:

A breakthrough is a new discovery with dramatic and far-reaching implications.

1. Christ-Centered people show enormous capacity for increased kingdom impact. Even the most devoted Christ Centered people fall far short of full devotion in both spiritual attitudes and behaviors. Bill Hybels consistently challenges Christians with the statement that "Ninety-five percent devotion to God falls 5 percent short." We believe this statement captures the essence of this great opportunity for the church. While the most dedicated Christ-followers are the best evangelists, volunteers and donors, we see evidence that they have a much greater capacity for spiritual engagement.

2. The Bible is the most powerful catalyst for spiritual growth. The Bible's power to advance spiritual growth is unrivaled by anything else we've discovered. Reflection on Scripture is by far the most influential spiritual practice, and it is also the only factor out of the more than fifty we assessed that appears on the list of top five catalysts for each of the three spiritual movements. That's why we conclude that it is the catalyst most predictive of spiritual growth.

Let's take a closer look at the evidence that provides the basis for these breakthrough observations.

CHRIST-CENTERED PEOPLE SHOW ENORMOUS CAPACITY FOR INCREASED KINGDOM IMPACT

The journey to becoming Christ-Centered is infinite; because we aspire to the perfect standard of Jesus Christ, our imperfect human lives will always fall short of that goal. This can be discouraging if you think about that gap as a set of impossible expectations. But from the standpoint of a senior church leader, this is an open door to a great opportunity—and that is to unapologetically raise the bar of expectations for spiritual engagement to increasingly higher levels.

Virtually all Christ-followers miss the 100 percent devotion standard by a considerable margin.

Our research shows virtually all Christ-followers miss the 100 percent devotion standard by a considerable margin—including those who consider themselves truly Christ-Centered. There are significant gaps—between what the Bible teaches and what our findings reveal—that should encourage senior church leaders to have no reservations about setting the challenge factor very high.

Consider the *heart* of the matter—the gap between the two attributes we use to define spiritual growth: love of God and love of others (Matthew 22:37–39) (chart 5-1).

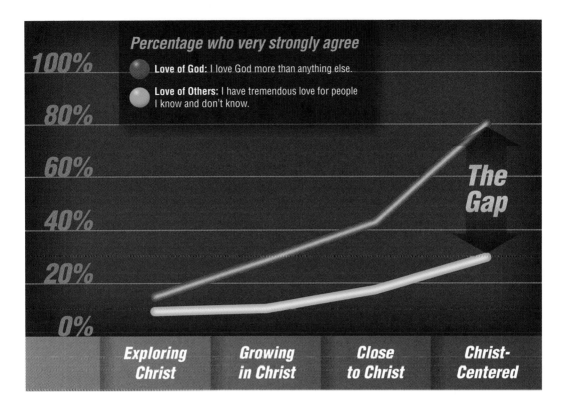

Attitudes about Loving God and Loving Others Show an Increasing Gap

Percentage who very strongly agree

Love of God: I love God more than anything else.

Love of Others: I have tremendous love for people I know and don't know.

100%

80%

60%

40%

20%

0%

The Gap

Exploring Christ   *Growing in Christ*   *Close to Christ*   *Christ-Centered*

Chart 5-1: The percentage of people who "very strongly agree" with statements about "love of God" and "love of others" rises across the spiritual continuum. However, there is a growing gap between those who "very strongly agree" with each statement across the continuum, meaning that people are more likely to "very strongly agree" with "love of God" than "love of others."

The top line tracks the increasing percentage across the spiritual continuum of those who responded "very strongly agree" to the statement "I love God more than anything else." Not surprisingly, that percentage climbs steeply for the more advanced segments. Note, however, that only 78 percent of the Christ-Centered people "very strongly agree" with this statement—which means that 22 percent chose answers reflecting lower degrees of commitment.

The most noteworthy gap exists in the comparison between the "love of God" responses and the lower line, which represents the percentage who "very strongly agree" that "I have tremendous love for people I know and don't know." The "love of God" percentage (78 percent) is more than two-and-a-half times higher than the "love of others" percentage (30 percent) for the Christ-Centered segment. Equally important, the gap between these two statements in the Christ-Centered segment is the largest on the spiritual continuum. In other words, the most mature Christ-followers report a greater distance between their "love of God" and "love of others" than any other segment. So, while the Christ-Centered people are fired up with their "love of God," their "love of others" trails far behind.

The generally low trajectory of "love of others" is a bit surprising.

Independent of its comparison with the "love of God" responses, the generally low trajectory of "love of others" is a bit surprising. Less than 20 percent of all other segments "very strongly agree" with the statement about loving others. With the media so full of stories about people stepping up to support the victims of domestic and international crises, it might seem reasonable to expect a "love of others" measure to track higher—regardless of a person's faith. The fact that Christians from the more advanced segments—Close to Christ and Christ-Centered—responded to this statement at such relatively low levels should be a cause for some soul-searching among church leaders.

This weaker picture for "love of others" is reinforced by serving patterns that climb across the spiritual continuum but also show that a greater serving capacity exists (chart 5-2).

Some Good News

The good news is that the percentage of people reporting that they serve monthly does rise across the spiritual continuum in the three capacities measured on the chart. Over 60 percent of the Christ-Centered segment serve at least once a month in a church ministry; 50 percent serve those in need "on my own" (outside the church) at least monthly; and over 30 percent serve those in need through their church once a month or more. Not surprisingly, there's quite a bit of overlap among these groups, meaning that people who serve those in need through the church also serve in church ministries. There are also a number of people who serve in one capacity, like serving those in need "on my own," but don't serve otherwise. When we net out the serving numbers, 83 percent of the Christ-Centered group serves in some kind of capacity at least once a month.

The bad news is that close to 40 percent don't serve in a church ministry once a month; 50 percent don't serve those in need "on my own" every month; and close to 70 percent don't serve those in need through the church at least once a month. When we look at total net serving, 17 percent of Christ-Centered people don't serve in any of these capacities once a month. These are significant numbers, especially for people who are Christ-Centered.

Monthly Serving Patterns Show a Gap

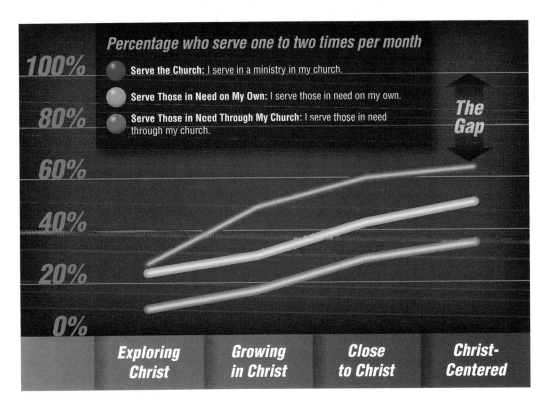

Chart 5-2: The percentage of people who report serving in some capacity at least once a month increases across the continuum. We would expect the Christ-Centered group to report very high serving levels, but there is a significant gap between 100 percent participation and actual participation in serving activities.

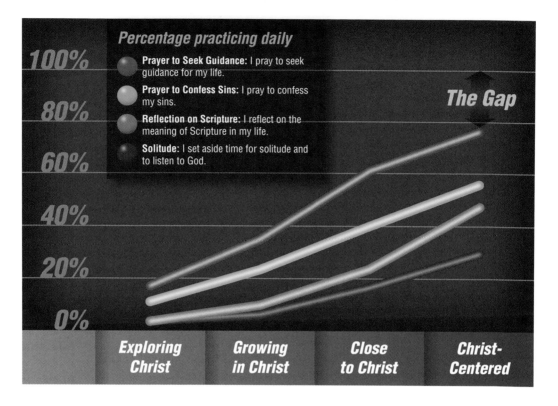

Personal Spiritual Practices Show a Gap

Percentage practicing daily

Prayer to Seek Guidance: I pray to seek guidance for my life.

Prayer to Confess Sins: I pray to confess my sins.

Reflection on Scripture: I reflect on the meaning of Scripture in my life.

Solitude: I set aside time for solitude and to listen to God.

The Gap

100%
80%
60%
40%
20%
0%

| Exploring Christ | Growing in Christ | Close to Christ | Christ-Centered |

Chart 5-3: The percentage of people who report daily personal spiritual practices increases across the continuum. We would expect the Christ-Centered group to report very high levels of daily spiritual practices, and they do. But there is a surprising gap between 100 percent participation in daily practices and their actual practice.

How to expand the heart is the challenge.

We should not take these findings as license to pressure people into greater serving commitments. This is not an issue about activity levels; it is an issue of the heart. In light of the lower "love for others" results, the relatively high percentages of Christ-followers who don't serve once a month suggests that this is a spiritual growth challenge. It also suggests that expanding people's hearts to embrace "love of others" as a faith value equivalent to "love of God" could generate substantial gains for the kingdom. How to expand the heart is the challenge—one that goes beyond merely increasing serving activity levels.

Personal spiritual practices may offer one remedy for expanding hearts (chart 5-3). As we've noted, a pattern of increased personal spiritual practices is highly correlated with increasing spiritual attitudes and behaviors across the spiritual continuum.

It's difficult to imagine a Christ-Centered person not experiencing daily prayer. But our research tells us that over 20 percent do not pray daily "to seek guidance for my life" and half do not "reflect on the meaning of Scripture in my life" on a daily basis. In human terms, this is the equivalent of choosing not to communicate with a spouse every day even though communication channels are readily available. Communication and shared experiences lie at the heart of most relationships. The closer the relationship, the more frequent the contact. These numbers suggest that opportunities to encourage greater intimacy with God through more frequent spiritual practices exist across the spiritual continuum, including in the Christ-Centered segment.

Over 20 percent of those who are Christ-Centered do not pray daily.

We can break down this opportunity to challenge the Christ-Centered even further by dividing them into two groups: committed and not committed.

Committed
Fifty percent of the Christ-Centered group said they "very strongly agree" with the statement that "I am willing to give up all that is important in my life for Jesus Christ."

Not committed
Fifty percent of the Christ-Centered group *did not* "very strongly agree" that "I am willing to give up all that is important in my life for Jesus Christ."

The two segments on the right of chart 5-4 represent subgroups of the Christ-Centered segment. The most important group on this chart is the one at the far right—the 50 percent of the Christ-Centered segment who answered "very strongly agree" to the statement "I am willing to risk everything that is important in my life for Jesus Christ." These are the Christ-Centered people who we call the most "committed."

Even when we focus on the committed—those who are willing to risk everything for Jesus—there are still 40 percent who don't tithe,

Even Those Who Are Most Committed to Christ
Show Surprising Gaps in Spiritual Practices and Activities

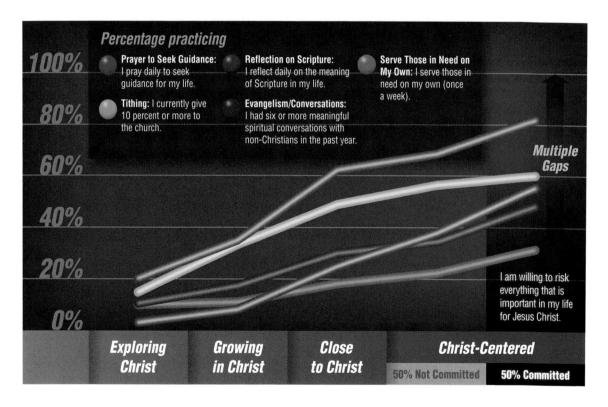

Chart 5-4: Dividing the Christ-Centered segment into two subgroups shows that even the most committed Christ-Centered people report gaps between what we would expect from those who are truly Christ-Centered and their actual practice and activity levels.

20 percent who don't pray daily "to seek guidance in my life," and 50 percent who have fewer than six spiritual conversations per year with non-believers. Although they do more serving, evangelizing, tithing, praying and Bible reflection than any other segment, they still have room to grow. They can still be challenged to serve the kingdom, and in general, they are inspired by their great love of God to want to do just that.

What's needed?

It may be as simple as issuing the challenge to pursue new and deeper levels of commitment and devotion to Christ. The heart is there. The right motivations are in place. But sometimes achieving the next level requires an encouraging challenge—the kind of challenge that coaches often provide for their best players.

In a nutshell, that's the opportunity for the church—to become a coach for the Christ-Centered people. Coaches are most effective when they help players see what they can't see in themselves—those big and small shifts that have the greatest potential to change momentum. The church can inspire and engage committed Christ-followers and hold them accountable for closing the gap between where they are and 100 percent devotion to Christ.

We want to challenge those who are already Christ-Centered to higher levels of devotion and commitment.

Our earliest research spoke to the great potential of the Christ-Centered segment. At that time, we focused exclusively on the opportunity to inspire as many people as possible to become Christ-Centered—to increase the number of people within this most highly engaged segment.

Now we see the potential of the Christ-Centered as something that is exponentially greater. Not only do we want to increase the number of Christ-Centered people; we also want to challenge those who are already Christ-Centered to higher levels of devotion and commitment. If they meet that challenge—and we have every confidence they will—the kingdom rewards could be significant.

THE BIBLE IS THE MOST POWERFUL CATALYST FOR SPIRITUAL GROWTH

In our earliest research, we concluded that the power of personal spiritual practices to advance spiritual growth is extraordinary, having arguably more influence on spiritual movement than anything else, including church activities. This finding inspired us to explore personal spiritual practices in much greater depth so we could gain more insight on the spiritual practices that are most significant at different points along the spiritual journey.

Spending time in the Bible is hands down the highest impact personal spiritual practice.

Everywhere we turned the data revealed the same truth: spending time in the Bible is hands down the highest impact personal spiritual practice. More specifically, "I reflect on the meaning of Scripture in my life" is the spiritual practice that is most predictive of growth for all three spiritual movements (chart 5-5).

There's great significance in the word *reflection*. Reflecting on Scripture implies a contemplative process, one of thoughtful and careful deliberation. This practice of "reflecting on the meaning of Scripture in my life" is about using God's Word as a mirror that reflects back the truth of Scripture on the actions, decisions and events of one's daily life. This is not about skimming through a Bible passage or devotional in a mechanical way. This is a powerful experience of personal meditation that catalyzes spiritual growth, starting at the very beginning of the spiritual journey.

One of the more intriguing findings is that reflection on Scripture is the most predictive personal spiritual practice in Movement 1. In our most recent research, we were able to assess the impact of first cracking open the Bible—in other words, the impact of increasing how often (from rarely to frequently) one reads the Bible and/or reflects on Scripture. Reflection on Scripture is the most influential spiritual practice in the earliest movement of spiritual growth, more so even than prayer, which may seem like a more logical high-impact spiritual practice for early believers.

Reflection on Scripture Is the Most Influential Spiritual Practice Across All Three Movements

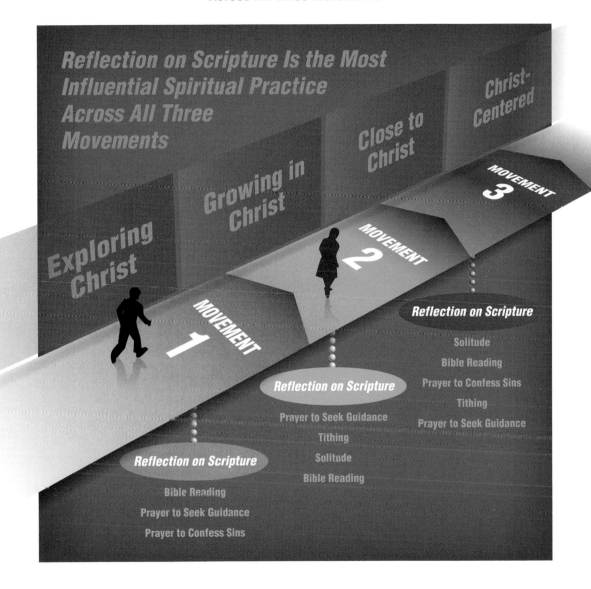

Chart 5-5: "Reflection on Scripture" is the most influential personal spiritual practice for all three spiritual movements.

Importantly, reflection on Scripture is also the only spiritual catalyst that appears on the list of top five factors for all three movements. When we threw all fifty-plus catalysts into the mix to assess which top five factors were the most influential catalysts of spiritual growth, reflection on Scripture was the only factor that appeared on all three lists (chart 5-6).

This is why we say the Bible is the most powerful catalyst of spiritual growth—similar to what I refer to as the "vanilla factor" in chapter 3 (page 53). Not only is reflection on Scripture head and shoulders above any other spiritual practice for all three movements when we assessed spiritual practices independently, but when we considered everything to determine the top five most influential factors, it surfaced on every list. That's remarkable. The Bible's influence seems to transcend all other factors—much like vanilla ice cream's popularity dwarfs all other flavors. The Bible is not just the vanilla when we look at personal spiritual practices; it's the vanilla when we look at *everything*.

We can consider the implications of this finding by thinking about another personal activity—one we all know is very good for our physical health, but not one we

The Bible's influence seems to transcend all other factors.

Reflection on Scripture Is the Only Factor That Appears in the Top Five Catalysts for All Three Movements

Exploring Christ to Growing in Christ

Movement 1

1. **Salvation by Grace** (Spiritual Belief/Attitude)
2. **The Trinity** (Spiritual Belief/Attitude)
3. **Serve the Church** (Church Activity)
4. **Prayer to Seek Guidance** (Spiritual Practice)
5. **Reflection on Scripture** (Spiritual Practice)

Growing in Christ to Close to Christ

Movement 2

1. **Personal God** (Spiritual Belief/Attitude)
2. **Prayer to Seek Guidance** (Spiritual Practice)
3. **Reflection on Scripture** (Spiritual Practice)
4. **Solitude** (Spiritual Practice)
5. **Evangelism** (Spiritual Activity with Others)

Close to Christ to Christ-Centered

Movement 3

1. **Giving Away My Life** (Spiritual Belief/Attitude)
2. **Christ Is First** (Spiritual Belief/Attitude)
3. **Identity in Christ** (Spiritual Belief/Attitude)
4. **Authority of the Bible** (Spiritual Belief/Attitude)
5. **Reflection on Scripture** (Spiritual Practice)

Chart 5-6: "Reflection on Scripture" is the only spiritual catalyst that appears on each list of "top five spiritual catalysts" for all three spiritual movements.

necessarily engage in as often as we should: exercise. There are typically two reasons why people don't exercise: they can't fit it into their weekly routine, or they don't enjoy it (it's boring or painful). Given the barriers, why do so many people still exercise regularly? They do it because they are aware of its health benefits. They know that out of all the things they might do to improve their health, nothing beats regular exercise.

Reflection on Scripture shares similar barriers—it doesn't always make it on the calendar, and we sometimes avoid it because we don't enjoy it. Like the exercise metaphor, it's possible that just raising awareness of its spiritual benefits might motivate people to adjust their daily routines to make room for reflection on Scripture. Based on our research, that action alone would offer the same magnitude of benefit to spiritual growth as exercise does to physical health.

Is your congregation fully aware of the importance of reflection on Scripture for their spiritual health? Do they know that nothing beats time spent in the Bible in terms of its power to advance spiritual growth? Are they aware that no matter where they are on their spiritual journey that nothing matters more to their spiritual development—including church services, serving activities, small groups—than time spent in God's Word? *Nothing* beats the Bible.

NOTHING beats the Bible.

When it comes to the second barrier—lack of enjoyment—it may take more than awareness to help people establish a routine practice. The translations of ancient texts with their unconventional language and unusual settings can feel inaccessible, especially for early believers. They approach those texts with caution and a little foreboding, similar to a novice exerciser's response to the rows of intimidating workout machines at the health club. It's possible that at times even our most advanced Christ-followers open their Bibles more out of habit than anticipation, just like those who routinely exercise get worn down by the monotony of hopping on the treadmill day after day.

Although there is no shortage of Bible primers, study guides, devotionals and other products to help guide us through the pages of Scripture, we should spare no creative juices when it comes to resources that unlock the mystery and power of God's Word for his people. The Bible does not share the grim monotony of the treadmill; it does not need to be a grinding routine. Overcoming this expectation—that time in the Bible is about as pleasant as lifting barbells—could go a long way toward accelerating spiritual growth for early believers, and even those who are more established in their faith. Remember that only half of our most committed Christ-followers reflect on Scripture every day (chart 5-4, page 112).

Awareness and *accessibility* are two key strategic opportunities for encouraging more people to engage in consistent Scripture reflection. *Challenge* and *coaching* are the two watchwords for inspiring Christ-Centered people to higher levels of spiritual engagement. These concepts aren't revolutionary or complicated. You don't need your congregation to take a survey to consider the implications of these findings for your church. In fact, we encourage you to take these observations and run with them! Whatever you can do to inspire Christ-Centered people to new levels of spiritual engagement or accelerate the start of new personal routines of reflection on Scripture, rest assured the kingdom benefits will be significant.

THE CHURCH AS COACH

The church's greatest role is that of spiritual motivator or spiritual coach.

As we reflect back over four years of gathering, studying and analyzing data on spiritual growth and the breakthroughs we've discovered, we believe that perhaps the church's greatest role is that of spiritual motivator or spiritual coach. The church can hold up a mirror to our souls that helps us see what we can't see for ourselves—all those big and small shifts that have the greatest potential to change our spiritual momentum. Like a coach, the church can help us create a spiritual workout plan. It can nudge us to run a little faster, or lift a few more weights. But mostly, the church's job—and its greatest joy—is to step back and cheer us on as the Holy Spirit captivates our hearts and uses us to do his mighty work.

It is our most sincere hope that what we discover through this research will make the church's spiritual coaching job much easier, and the output from that labor much more fruitful.

GREG L. HAWKINS

6

CHANGES AT WILLOW

GOING FROM INCREMENTAL IMPROVEMENT TO
RETHINKING CORE STRATEGY

bold decisions

IF TRANSFORMATION IS THE GOAL, tinkering and tweaking just won't cut it. Discover the three changes Willow is embarking on, as well as insights about how to catalyze spiritual movement in your church.

6

CHANGES AT WILLOW

One year ago, we published *Reveal*. In it, we presented findings from our three-year study on how spiritual growth really happens. In the final chapter, I mentioned three specific changes Willow was pursuing to respond to what we had learned:

> 1. *Our message to the congregation has to change.*
>
> 2. *We need to coach next steps.*
>
> 3. *We need to extend the impact of our weekend services.*

What we've learned has inspired us to make some bold decisions.

Since then, we've surveyed hundreds of additional congregations and analyzed the results. What we've learned has not only increased our own understanding of what catalyzes spiritual movement, but has inspired us to make some bold decisions.

THE CONTEXT FOR CHANGE

The more insight we glean, the more we realize that the three changes we initially pursued aren't sufficient for stimulating and sustaining the sort of spiritual growth we want our people to experience. The changes have helped, but there is more that we want and need to do.

Recasting Our Primary Message

By way of context, the first of the three changes Willow believed necessary for catalyzing spiritual growth and development revolved around changing the primary message that we were delivering to our congregation. In effect, we had been telling our congregation for years, "We know what your spiritual needs are, and we believe we know the program or activity that can best meet those needs for you." We were wrong. A "one-size-fits-all" process was not what people needed. In April 2007, we began to recast our core message to have people "move from dependence *on* the church to a growing interdependent partnership *with* the church."[1] We learned the hard way that to expect a one-size-fits-all approach to meet each person's spiritual needs was just not realistic.

A "one-size-fits-all" process was not what people needed.

Coaching Next Steps

The second big change we identified involved coaching next steps. When surveyed, people said they came to Willow (and other churches) because they wanted to move forward spiritually. They wanted to know what next steps to take in their journey with God. In chapter 1, I describe this desire using the metaphor of going to a health club and working with a trainer who helps create a customized plan for physical growth. As a church, we wanted something of a spiritual equivalent to that, the ability to provide appropriate next steps for spiritual growth on a personalized basis. We began developing an online tool that individuals could use to assess where they are spiritually and recommend next steps. It was a lot harder to do than we thought. But the more we worked on it, the more we realized a tool by itself wasn't enough. We needed to incorporate next-step coaching into *everything* we did, beginning with our weekend services. More on that later.

[1] Greg L. Hawkins and Cally Parkinson, *Reveal* (Barrington, Ill.: Willow Creek Resources, 2007), 65.

Extending the Impact of Our Weekend Services

The third change we pursued was to extend the impact of our weekend services. We wanted to help people integrate what they were learning on the weekends into their Monday-through-Friday lives. For example, last year during two message series, one in the spring and one in the fall, we handed out journals. The journal provided a place for people to write their responses to thoughtful and compelling questions about the message content they'd heard on Sunday, and it listed reference books and other resources they could use for deeper study. It was a simple tool, but people told us it had a significant impact on their "between-Sundays" growth.

We Needed Bigger Changes

So, as I mentioned, we made progress on all of these changes, but as we began to live them out and after learning from the new research, we realized they were not going to be sufficient for catalyzing the kind of movement we wanted to see in the spiritual lives of our people. What we needed was a bigger set of changes.

What we needed was a bigger set of changes.

In addition to having lengthy discussions about which changes to pursue, we looked to other churches who were also gathering and responding to input from their congregations. These were the churches who had raised their hands and said, "Count us in" for the same kind of assessment Willow had gone through. We were curious about what we could learn from them.

During the fall of 2007, I went on the road to seven cities to teach a one-day seminar on what we were learning from our ongoing research. I wound up talking to more than a thousand church leaders, continuing the discussion about what works and what doesn't work in various settings. Those conversations became the early catalyst for three additional changes for Willow—changes we hope will catalyze even deeper spiritual growth within our congregation.

THREE CHANGES

The question we've been wracking our brains over recently is, *How do we build on Willow's historic strengths while embracing new spiritual growth practices going forward?* So far, our response includes making three changes:

1. *We need to become as radical in equipping believers to live Christ-Centered lives as we are at reaching seekers.*

2. *We need to morph our midweek service into a variety of "next step" learning opportunities.*

3. *We have to offer a broader portfolio of targeted experiences and resources to catalyze spiritual movement.*

1. We Need to Become as Radical in Equipping Believers to Live Christ-Centered Lives as We Are at Reaching Seekers

The often-undervalued truth of the seeker movement is that fully devoted followers of Christ always fueled it. The REVEAL data confirms this. Nothing new here. What is new and truly represents the real breakthrough of the REVEAL initiative is that we now have a powerful lens and framework to help churches move beyond inspiration to actual implementation of a focused, intentional strategy to equip people to live Christ-Centered lives.

During Willow's early days in the 1970s, it was nearly unheard of to invite someone far from God to church. We wanted to change that thinking. Three decades after that initial decision, we hope that we have played a role in redefining "normal" for thousands of churches all over the world who now plan and host weekend worship services that provide safe places for seekers to hear the dangerous message of Christ.

Our hearts will always burn for those far from God. But we now have an even deeper understanding about how crucial these Christ-Centered people are to the church—they are the engine that drives everything in our church. They have died to self and have oriented their values and their lifestyle around the person of Jesus Christ. They have yielded their souls to God so that he can use them to make a meaningful difference in this world. So the church must do more than give lip service to equipping believers. Everyone says they do this, but we now know most churches don't—including churches that say they are all about this and would not describe themselves as seeker sensitive.

We now have an even deeper understanding about how crucial these Christ-Centered people are to the church.

Challenge Them to Become Disciples

Faithful followers of Christ need to know that they're not crazy. They need to see that their church stands behind them. They need to be honored for their sacrifice. They need to be challenged not to serve the church's agenda, but to serve Christ's agenda in the world. As a result of our shift in focus, we are reevaluating and realigning our ministry activity so that Christ-Centered people are trained to value Christ-Centered living above all human agendas. We are asking new questions, like, "Is this ministry more about the church's agenda or the person's progress toward Christ-Centered living?"

Equip Them to Make Disciples

Once a person becomes a disciple, he or she is then instructed to go make more disciples, to reach out to those who don't know God (Matthew 28:19–20). Interestingly, all of our research suggests that Christ-Centered people evangelize whether the church encourages it or not. They have conversations with people far from God. They invite them to church. They pray for them. They try to help them take next steps in their lives. They echo Paul's sentiment in Acts 20:24, considering their lives worth nothing if only they may finish the race and complete the task the Lord Jesus has given them, the task of testifying to the gospel of God's grace. Our desire is to equip these Christ-Centered people to go and make disciples more consistently, more effectively and with greater resources behind them.

Our desire is to equip these Christ-Centered people to go and make disciples more effectively.

"Equipping" can mean different things for different people. Some need to be trained to disciple less-mature believers. Some need to be taught how to lead an effective small group. Some need resources so they can serve their neighbors who fall on hard times or help out schoolchildren from low-income families who could really use backpacks and school clothes. Some will need to be released so that HIV/AIDS orphans in Africa can be cared for and educated.

From a church strategy point of view, REVEAL gives us specific knowledge about the changing needs people have and what is spiritually catalytic as believers progress toward Christ-Centered living. That knowledge is driving the development of a focused strategy that better cooperates with the Holy Spirit's transforming work in people's lives.

2. We Need to Morph Our Midweek Service into a Variety of "Next Step" Learning Opportunities

The second major change we are making impacts our worship service structure. For more than thirty years, we have used our weekend services to present the truths of Christianity on a basic level that anyone could understand so that our core attenders had a safe and predictable place to bring their unchurched friends. At the same time, this service has also been designed to challenge believers.

In addition to attending weekend services, we encouraged people who had already made the decision to follow Christ to come back during the middle of the week for an extended time of worship and more advanced Bible teaching.

The idea was that, no matter where you were in your spiritual journey, you could come to the weekend service or the midweek service or both services, and have an opportunity to experience God and receive great Bible-based teaching. But what if where you were in your spiritual life was not served by either of those events, no matter how well they were delivered?

Certainly, teaching from the Bible never returns void. We wouldn't dispute that. But in thinking about what is most catalytic for moving someone toward a Christ-Centered life, we are now convinced we've got to give people more options than those two preset teaching times.

REVEAL gives us specific knowledge about the changing needs people have.

Very soon, our midweek service will change. We will still have a time of corporate worship, but instead of everyone then listening to the same teaching, they will disperse to one of a variety of smaller classes or other learning experiences. Some classes will be designed for those who are Exploring Christ and will feature the kinds of information and experiences that help those early in the journey take a next step. Other classes will focus on helping people learn and practice spiritual disciplines like solitude, prayer or journaling. Still others will be designed to ground people in the core beliefs of the Christian faith. The key is, there will be opportunities for everyone—regardless of where they are on the spiritual continuum—to learn, grow and take next steps toward becoming more like Christ.

As content is developed for each learning opportunity, our desire is to capture as much of it as possible in a searchable online library so that we can make it available to members of the congregation who were unable to attend a particular class. The research makes it clear that people want to take advantage of a variety of next-step opportunities. Additionally, we will ask participants to reflect on how well each experience served their spiritual movement and to log those responses. Over time, we will be able to recommend the right resources for the right person at the right stage of their spiritual journey.

3. We Have to Offer a Broader Portfolio of Targeted Experiences and Resources to Catalyze Spiritual Movement

The third change we have agreed to make is that we will provide experiences and resources beyond weekend services and midweek opportunities that can stimulate and encourage growth in Christ-followers at all points on the spiritual continuum—Exploring Christ, Growing in Christ, Close to Christ, and Christ-Centered.

People come to church because they want to grow. They recognize something is missing in their lives, they see something more they desire and they enter our buildings in hopes of closing that gap. They don't want to leave empty-handed. Instead, they want to leave our company knowing they have moved, that they now know what they must work on to get closer to their desired destination. We know this is the goal for those who walk through our doors. We also know this goal won't be met if people just spend a couple of hours at church each week.

People come to church because they want to grow.

Two Types of Experiences

Although we'll suggest experiences in conjunction with our weekend services and midweek learning opportunities, we believe there are two types of experiences that must be offered on an intentional and ongoing basis: experiences to build community, and experiences to promote Christlike service.

Experiences to Build Community

The Christian life was never meant to be lived in isolation. We need each other. Furthermore, we firmly believe that life change can happen best in the context of biblical community. But biblical community has many forms, and the form that's necessary for a given person may depend on where they are on the spiritual continuum.

Perhaps an example will help to illustrate this point. When I was new to the Christian faith, it was very important for me to feel heard and to have my questions answered. The type of community I needed was a structured Bible study with other men. After my wife and I got married a few years later, it was helpful to be in a small group with other married couples so that I could learn how to apply my faith to my new relationship.

As I grew spiritually over the years, I moved into a leadership role with various small groups. And now, as I mature even more in my relationship with Christ, I tend to seek out community experiences that are

While it's true that everybody needs to be "in community," the form that community takes may look different depending on their spiritual maturity level.

equally challenging and helpful to my growth but far less structured than the ones I looked for twenty years ago.

In the past, leaders at Willow told people that everybody needed to be in a church-organized small group. We're reframing that message to convey that, while it's true that everybody needs to be "in community," the form that community takes may look different depending on their spiritual maturity level. One person who is exploring Christ might benefit most from being in a formal seeker small group, while another might just need to connect with a spiritual friend. One Christ-Centered person might want the structure of a weekly Bible study curriculum, while another might say, "I want more of a relational group I can go deep with, a place where I can share my struggles and receive accountability and wisdom in return."

It's not feasible for us as a church to put everybody who's looking to be mentored in contact with everybody who's willing to mentor. It's just not practical. But if you were to release a few hundred Christ-Centered people from the responsibility of participating in or leading a small group every year and instead encourage them to find an outlet for community in which they could reach out and help people who are younger in their faith, you can't imagine the mentoring inroads that would be made. This is just one example of what we believe a "portfolio of community experiences" will afford us in terms of freedom and growth.

Experiences to Encourage Christlike Service

The second kind of experience we want to provide revolves around acts of service. Willow Creek has always offered a broad base of serving experiences—from on-campus experiences that help meet the basic needs of running the church, to off-campus experiences that meet needs in our community and around the world. And our people are among the most servant-oriented folks we have surveyed. However, now that we know how catalytic serving really is for a person's spiritual growth, we want to put even more emphasis on serving, especially on serving those in need.

Resources to Reinforce Key Learnings

In addition to experiences, we need to offer resources. For the past decade or more, we have been capturing every weekend and midweek message in a digital format that is easily uploaded to our web site. In our bookstore we have shelves of helpful books, stacks of useful group-based training and hundreds of DVDs that can help a person move from Exploring Christ to becoming Christ-Centered.

We are in the process of cataloging every resource we carry and categorizing each one according to how we think it will help someone grow. For example, we want to determine the best resources to help someone move from Exploring Christ to Growing in Christ (Movement 1). We want to organize and present resources that way and then ask people to evaluate how helpful the resources actually are in helping them grow spiritually. Over time, we will revise our recommendations based on the feedback we get.

We recognize that this undertaking will require a major investment in our digital infrastructure. But it's worth it to us to be able to provide tried and true recommendations to people about the next message they need to hear or the next book they need to read in order to get where God is inviting them to go.

✦ ✦ ✦

If the only thing you look at are the format changes, Willow's new approach may not seem all that substantial. For decades, most churches have had one weekend service, taught classes and provided a variety of experiences and resources for their congregations. So what's the big deal?

For Willow Creek Community Church, these changes are significant because they're not just about format. They're about *radical intentionality*—making sure that everything we do creates spiritual movement, thereby enabling us to accomplish our mission of turning irreligious people into fully devoted followers of Jesus Christ. I am excited to share with you what we discover in the days and years to come. Something tells me our learning has just begun.

These changes are significant because they're not just about format.

THE SUM TOTAL OF OUR WORK

The most frequently asked question I've received from pastors in recent months is, "What's the most significant thing you have learned from all of this research?" Then they stare at me with baited breath, braced for the silver bullet I'm about to fire their way so they can painlessly and effortlessly go fix their church. And I imagine my response is a bit of a disappointment every time.

"Well, like I have said before, the research clearly indicates that we need to do a better job equipping the Christ-Centered group and we need to help all people engage more deeply with the Bible.

"But there's a deeper answer to your question," I continue. "The one great takeaway from our work thus far is that God is *ridiculously* in love with us. That's it. God loves us! And his Holy Spirit is working to draw

In 2007, the REVEAL database included 5,000 people from seven churches. The findings in *Follow Me* are based on surveys from 80,000 people in 200 churches—and the numbers are still growing. Today, the REVEAL database includes 157,000 people from over 500 churches. Our original findings have been confirmed and greatly enriched by the depth and diversity of this database. It is our hope that the 500 churches feel similarly enriched by the insights discovered about their congregations through their participation in the REVEAL Spiritual Life Survey.

We have come a long way, but we realize that this is just the beginning. What we know now is the tip of the iceberg compared to what we want to know and what we believe the Spiritual Life Survey has the potential to uncover. Here are some of the areas we hope to explore in future research.

"Best in Class" Churches

Our dream is to help every church learn from the churches that are most effective at advancing spiritual growth. Upcoming REVEAL events and resources will highlight our findings about the activities and processes of "best in class" churches. Visit the REVEAL web site for more information about new events and resources:

www.revealnow.com

The Missing Movement

What draws people to God in the first place? In chapter 3 we acknowledged a "missing movement," which is the transition from being Far from God to Exploring Christ. In the days ahead, we hope to reach beyond church walls and gather input from those who are unchurched so we can identify the spiritual catalysts that are most influential to taking the first steps toward faith.

Students

Why do so many young people fall away from their faith after the high school years? We want to gain a better understanding of the spiritual growth experience for junior high and high school students so we can identify the greatest opportunities for cementing their faith before they leave home.

Christian Community

We have struggled to fully understand the impact that Christian community has on spiritual development with the REVEAL survey results to date. Our analysis so far suggests that spiritual beliefs, personal practices and activities like serving or evangelism are more catalytic to spiritual growth. We want to take a deeper dive, both qualitatively and quantitatively, into how the dynamics of Christian community are interwoven with these catalysts to contribute to movement throughout the spiritual journey.

Long-Term Goals

One of our long-term goals is international expansion, but we think we need a little more experience under our belts with domestic churches before we include churches in countries beyond the United States and Canada.

Another long-term goal is longitudinal research, which means surveying the same people using the same measures at different points in time. Specifically, we want to track individual spiritual growth experiences over time so we can gain a more thorough understanding of the direct cause-and-effect relationship between spiritual catalysts and spiritual movement. Ideally we would like to enrich our understanding of spiritual movement by following the spiritual growth path of specific individuals rather than relying exclusively on point-in-time research done with large groups (see appendix 2, "Research Approach and Methodology," page 144). ◆

us closer to him—sometimes with the assistance of a local church, but many times *in spite of* the local church."

I go on to explain that our team has studied a wide range of churches—small churches and large, seeker-focused and not, denominational and independent and so forth. But amid the variety, we see a common thread weaving its way through them all: there are people in every congregation who really do hunger and thirst after righteousness; who love God with their whole heart, mind and strength; and who have laid themselves at the feet of Jesus and said, "Use me however you wish to use me. Whatever that looks like, I'm in." You can feel it coming off the pages of the data. And that's a very good thing.

The Bible's claim about God being insanely in love with us is completely true.

But simultaneously, although we've seen some churches whose systems and practices are wildly effective for an individual's spiritual growth, we've observed too many churches that appear less than effective in catalyzing people's movement toward Christ.

The only conclusion I can come to, then, is that the Bible's claim about God being insanely in love with us is completely true. You see, whether people are in a great church, a good church or a struggling church, we have always found large numbers of people being drawn toward a deep intimacy with Christ. God is actively at work, with or without the help of the particular church someone attends. He is not willing to lose even one of us.

At the end of the day, the sum total of our work is not another set of charts and graphs and analysis, helpful though those things can be. Fundamentally, this work is about *love*. Fundamentally, this work centers on the story of a God who is so outrageously in love with his people that he will do whatever he must do in order for us to experience communion with him and co-labor with him in accomplishing his redemptive work in the world.

REAL CHANGE BEGINS
WITH YOU

I believe that if you take this work seriously—if you read this book carefully, and if you go beyond that to have your own church surveyed using the Spiritual Life Survey tool,[2] and if you interact with the results you find—you'll figure out what you need to do differently in your church. I am convinced that the Spirit of God will speak to you and that you will discern what you need to do in your particular setting.

But I also believe that real change will stick only when you as the leader treat your personal development with equal seriousness. In talking with hundreds of pastors whose churches are thriving even in the midst of great change, we have become convinced that their strong self-leadership is the key to their success.

Strong self-leaders examine themselves and answer the tough questions with boldness, questions like . . .

1. *Where am I?*

2. *Where do I want to be?*

3. *What's next for me?*

They figure out their next steps, they wrestle with God in prayer over how to prioritize their busy lives and they do what they need to do so they can become even more surrendered to Christ.

2 For more information, see appendix 4, "What Is the REVEAL Spiritual Life Survey?" on page 156.

I have all the confidence in the world that we will take appropriate next steps to help our churches get better. The real question I have as a pastor myself is whether we'll take the next steps for our souls. And more personally, will I take the steps I know I must take?

Are you willing to be awakened to what God has for you?

What step do you need to take to get closer to Christ today? What step do you need to take to let go of something that's holding onto your heart? What next step will unify your spirit, so that you can serve Christ and Christ alone? Are you willing to be awakened to what God has for you?

FACE-TO-FACE WITH JESUS

One of the children's books I read to my kids tells the Bible story of the blind man Bartimaeus. Jesus is walking through town one day, and although Bartimaeus can't see what's going on, he hears the roars of the crowd and knows that it must be something big. He pleads for information at the top of his voice and in response hears the people say, "Jesus is coming! Jesus is coming!"

When the shouts of the crowd reach fever pitch, Bartimaeus yells out to Jesus, "Come help me! Please . . . help me!"

Jesus comes to Bartimaeus's side and heals him. Bartimaeus opens his once-blind eyes and sees the sunshine and the countryside and the people who had been cheering and shouting all around him. Then, finally, Bartimaeus sees Jesus.

I start to cry every time I read that part of the story because, more than anything else, that's what I want for myself. I want to be so close to Jesus Christ that when I look up, I see him face-to-face. I want to meet his gaze and see his pleasure. I want to be reminded that nearness to him means that everything else will be okay. I'll be okay. My church will be okay. My marriage will be okay. My kids will be okay. *All* of life will be okay, as long as I stay close.

I think it's what our congregations want too.

And it all starts with having our own eyes opened first.

You see, this isn't about building a great church. It's about building a great Church. We're inviting people on a journey to be completely one with Christ, to be so close to him that we could look up from a prayer time or a worship event or a service opportunity and see his face clearly enough that we can actually make out the words on his lips:

Follow me! I will show you the way.

I know you.

I love you.

You were made

for this relationship.

And this is where you belong.

Bill Hybels

AFTERWORD: PURSUING A CHRIST-CENTERED STRATEGY

In 2004, Willow staff members Greg Hawkins and Cally Parkinson and research advisor Eric Arnson suggested that we do an in-depth, churchwide survey that could potentially impact the structural and systemic landscape at Willow. Their idea was to gather information from our entire congregation in order to assess how well we were (or were not) helping people grow spiritually. Although I had no idea what awaited us on the other side of the research, I believed God was calling us to pursue it. So we signed up.

It is in our DNA to "do church better" and to share what we learn with the greater church community.

It is in our DNA to "do church better" and to share what we learn with the greater church community. When God blesses something at Willow, we give him the credit and spread the story to any interested church leader. When we attempt something and fail miserably, we try to warn other leaders before they pay the same price we paid. We've been told that our transparency has been appreciated.

When our survey results indicated that Willow had significant room to improve the way we coach people toward full devotion to Christ, we published our findings to the wider kingdom, rolled up our sleeves and went to work. While some bloggers spent their time sensationalizing misleading headlines about our findings, we were busy trying to discern God's direction as to how we could more effectively help believers move toward Christ-Centered living.

Over the years, God has led us to implement many new strategies, but the motivation for every strategy has remained unchanged: *to turn irreligious people into fully devoted followers of Christ*. In the youth ministry that gave birth to Willow Creek thirty-three years ago, we believed the best way to reach people far from God was to take a bunch of Christ-Centered high school kids and inspire and equip them to share the reality of their faith with their friends. So that's what we did.

In light of what we've learned from REVEAL, that still appears to be the most effective way to reach people far from God. Drawing on that confirmation of our original motivation, we have a renewed commitment to strengthening the efforts of the Christ-Centered people in our church through increased training in prayer, relationship building, and evangelism—as well as the availability of seeker-friendly events.

Today there are roughly four thousand people at Willow who claim to be sold out to God—heart, mind, body and soul. Data supports the fact that they pray more than anybody else prays. They serve more than anybody else serves. They give more than anybody else gives. They evangelize more than anybody else. "It's no longer about my dreams, my plans or my career," they say. "It's no longer about counting my life as dear to myself. It's about laying it down for Christ, again and again and again."

Humanly speaking, these are the folks who make things happen around Willow. They're probably the ones who make things happen in your church, too. If the REVEAL research to date has impressed one thing on me as a leader, it's this:

> *If the church doesn't harness and support the enthusiasm and engagement of Christ-Centered people, they'll bail.*

Not on God, but on us as churches—churches that obviously don't support the pursuit of Christ-Centeredness.

Who wants that?

We have a renewed commitment to strengthening the efforts of the Christ-Centered people in our church.

The best days of the local church are ahead of us.

Undoubtedly we'll be exploring the question of what it means to support Christ-Centeredness for months and years to come, but two things are obvious. First, Christ-Centered people need to be reminded that they're not crazy for taking Christianity so seriously. They need to be reminded of the Scriptures that tell all of us that making our lives a living sacrifice is a normal part of the Christian life.

Second, Christ-Centered people need resources. They are actively building relationships, sharing a verbal witness and helping their friends explore Christianity. They're learning more and more to die to self and to humbly do whatever Christ calls them to do. But many of them are asking, "Could we get a little help here?" Church leaders could lighten their load significantly by providing the resources, opportunities and tools they need to thrive in their calling as Christians. If we boldly lift up the vision of a Christ-Centered life, and do whatever it takes to equip our people to live out that kind of life, I believe the impact on people living far from God will be profound and unprecedented.

I am dreaming of the day when church leaders will be passionate enough to seek the truth about the spiritual health of their congregations and courageous enough to make the necessary changes. I can feel the beginnings of that kind of shift throughout the world. It bolsters my belief that the best days of the local church are ahead of us, and that the gates of hell had better be prepared for a steady retreat.

BILL HYBELS

Founding and Senior Pastor
Willow Creek Community Church

Chairman of the Board
Willow Creek Association

APPENDICES

appendix **1**

WHAT IS REVEAL?

A Research-Based View of the Spiritual Journey

REVEAL is a research-based view of how the spiritual journey unfolds, validated to date through survey input from over 157,000 congregants in more than 500 churches.[1] The distinction of REVEAL is its ability to "measure the unseen," using a research approach that assesses how people's spiritual attitudes, needs and motivations align with spiritual behaviors.

REVEAL identifies a spiritual continuum comprised of four segments of people at different stages of spiritual development: Exploring Christ, Growing in Christ, Close to Christ and Christ-Centered. REVEAL's deeper value, however, is found in its insights about what creates movement along the journey; for example, which church activities, beliefs, spiritual practices or activities (evangelism, serving, etc.) are most influential to spiritual growth at different points across the spiritual continuum.

A Book

Published in 2007, *Reveal: Where Are You?* describes the initial aggregate findings based on input from 5,000 surveys completed by seven different congregations. *Follow Me: What's Next for You?* expands on earlier findings about the four segments on the spiritual continuum by describing the spiritual catalysts most influential to movement along the continuum. The findings in *Follow Me* are based on input from 80,000 surveys completed by people in more than 200 congregations.

A Spiritual Life Survey

The Spiritual Life Survey is a research tool local churches can use to assess the spiritual health of their congregations. The goal of the Spiritual Life Survey is to provide church leaders with a research tool equivalent to the finest research tool used in the marketplace at a small fraction of the marketplace cost. For more information, see appendix 4, "What Is the REVEAL Spiritual Life Survey?" (page 156), or visit www.revealnow.com.

[1] For more information and a brief history of REVEAL, visit www.revealnow.com.

RESEARCH APPROACH AND METHODOLOGY

This project began with a simple question: Could scientific research help us understand and perhaps measure spiritual growth? In other words, could the same research tools used in the marketplace to measure consumer attitudes and behaviors also be used by local churches to measure the spiritual beliefs and behaviors of their congregations? We believed the answer was yes.

We have refined our research over the course of four years, more than 500 churches and 157,000 individual surveys. While we're still in the early phases of our work, we feel confident that the research survey tool has proven capable of producing valid and valuable insight for church leaders.

Here is a brief overview of our research approach and methodology.

Approach

Our approach focused on three key areas and questions related to those areas:

- **Segments:** What are the different groups/segments of people the church might be looking to serve?
- **Needs:** What spiritual growth needs are being met, not being met well or not being met at all for each segment?
- **Drivers and Barriers:** What are the drivers of spiritual growth, and what are the barriers to spiritual growth?

These three areas provided the framework around which we organized the information we collected.

Methodology

Broadly speaking, there are two types of research methodology: qualitative and quantitative. We used both qualitative and quantitative methodologies, and then employed analytical techniques and processes to review the data.

Qualitative (Gathering Insights)

This is typically a one-on-one process in which a researcher poses questions directly to an individual. The questions often ask not only for information and opinions but also allow the interviewer to probe the richness of emotions and motivations related to the topic. Researchers use qualitative data to help clarify hypotheses, beliefs, attitudes and motivations. Qualitative work is often a first step because it enables a researcher to fine-tune the language that will be used in quantitative tools.

Researchers use qualitative data to help clarify hypotheses, beliefs, attitudes and motivations.

Quantitative (Establishing Statistical Reliability)

This process utilizes detailed questionnaires often distributed to large numbers of people. Questions are typically multiple choice and participants choose the most appropriate response among those listed for each question. Quantitative research collects a huge amount of data, which can often be generalized to a larger population and allow for direct comparisons between two or more groups. It also provides statisticians with a great deal of flexibility in analyzing the results.

Analytical Process and Techniques (Quantifying Insights and Conclusions)

Quantitative research is followed by an analytical plan designed to process the data for information and empirically based insights. Three common analytical techniques were used in our three research phases:

- **Correlation Analysis:** Measures whether or not, and how strongly, two variables are related. This does not mean that one variable causes the other; it means they tend to follow a similar pattern of movement.
- **Discriminate Analysis:** Determines which variables best explain the differences between two or more groups. This does not mean the variables cause the differences to occur between the groups; it means the variables distinguish one group from another.
- **Regression Analysis:** Used to investigate relationships between variables. This technique is typically utilized to determine whether or not the movement of a defined (or dependent) variable is caused by one or more independent variables.

We used both qualitative and quantitative methods in 2004 when we focused exclusively on Willow Creek Community Church and also in our 2007–2008 research involving hundreds of churches. Here is a summary of the methodology used in our most recent work.

Qualitative Phase (December 2006)

- *One-on-one interviews with sixty-eight congregants.* We specifically recruited people in the more advanced stages of spiritual growth. Our goal was to capture language and insights to help guide the development of our survey questionnaire.

- *Interview duration:* 30–45 minutes

- *Focused on fifteen topics.* Topics included spiritual life history, church background, personal spiritual practices, spiritual attitudes and beliefs, etc.

Quantitative Phases

PHASE 1 (January–February 2007)

- E-mail survey fielded with seven churches diverse in geography, size, ethnicity and format

- Received 4,943 completed surveys

- Utilized fifty-three sets of questions on topics such as:
  - ✛ Attitudes about Christianity and one's personal spiritual life
  - ✛ Personal spiritual practices, including statements about frequency of Bible reading, prayer, journaling, etc.
  - ✛ Satisfaction with the role of the church in spiritual growth
  - ✛ Importance and satisfaction of specific church attributes (e.g., helps me understand the Bible in depth) related to spiritual growth
  - ✛ Most significant barriers to spiritual growth
  - ✛ Participation and satisfaction with church activities, such as weekend services, small groups, youth ministries and serving

PHASE 2 (April–May 2007)

- E-mail survey fielded with twenty-five churches diverse in geography, size, ethnicity and format

- Received 15,977 completed surveys

- Utilized a refined set of questions based on Phase 1 research

PHASE 3 (October–November 2007 and January–February 2008)

- E-mail survey fielded with 487 churches diverse in geography, size, ethnicity and format, including ninety-one churches in seventeen countries

- Received 136,547 completed surveys

- Utilized a refined set of questions based on Phase 2 research
  - ✛ Expanded survey to include twenty statements about core Christian beliefs and practices from *The Christian Life Profile Assessment Tool Training Kit.*[1]
  - ✛ Added importance and satisfaction measures for specific attributes related to weekend services, small groups, children's and youth ministries and serving experiences.

Analytical Process and Resources

Each phase of our research included an analytical plan executed by statisticians and research professionals. These plans utilized many analytical techniques, including correlation, discriminate and regression analyses. In this book, our observations about the predictability of spiritual factors are derived primarily from extensive discriminate analysis. To put our analytical approach into perspective, here are three points of explanation about the nature of our research philosophy.

1. Our research is a snapshot in time.

Because this research is intentionally done at one point in time—like a snapshot—it is impossible to determine with certainty that a given variable, such as reflection on Scripture, distinguishes one segment from another (for example, Growing in Christ compared with Close to Christ). To accomplish this, we would have to assess the spiritual development of the same people over a period of time (longitudinal research).

However, the fact that increased levels of reflection on Scripture occur in the Close to Christ segment compared with the Growing

---

[1] Randy Frazee, *The Christian Life Profile Assessment Tool Training Kit* (Grand Rapids, Mich.: Zondervan, 2005).

in Christ segment strongly suggests that reflection on Scripture does influence spiritual movement between these segments (Movement 2). While it does not determine conclusively that a given variable "causes" movement, discriminate analysis identifies the factors that are the most differentiating characteristics between the two segments. So we infer from its findings that certain factors are more "predictive" and consequently more influential to spiritual growth.

Our ultimate goal is to measure the same people over multiple points in time (longitudinal research) in order to more clearly understand the causal effects of spiritual growth. However, even then we know there will be much left to learn, and much we will never understand about spiritual formation. The attitudes and behaviors we measure today should not be misinterpreted as defining spiritual formation. Instead they should be considered instruments used by the Holy Spirit to open our hearts for his formative work.

2. The purpose of this research is to provide a diagnostic tool for local churches.

Our intent is to provide a diagnostic tool for churches that is equivalent to the finest marketplace research tool at a fraction of the marketplace cost. This is "applied" research rather than "pure" research, meaning that its intent is to provide actionable insights for church leaders, not to create social science findings for academic journals.

In a nutshell, while we intend to reinforce our research base with longitudinal studies, we chose to draw conclusions about the predictability and the influence of spiritual attitudes and behaviors based on point-in-time research evaluated through discriminate analysis. This approach meets the most rigorous standards of market research that routinely influence decision making at some of the most respected and successful organizations in the country.

3. Research is an art as well as a science.

While the data underlying our findings is comprehensive and compelling as *science*, we have also benefited from the *art* of experts whose judgment comes from years of experience. The two research experts closest to this work represent almost fifty years of wide-ranging applied research projects. Eric Arnson began his career in quantitative consumer science at Proctor & Gamble, and ultimately became the North American leader of brand strategy for McKinsey and Company. Terry Schweizer spent twenty years with the largest custom-market research organization in the world, running its Chicago office before contributing full time to the final development phases of REVEAL. Eric and Terry poured the benefit of their expertise and judgment into every finding in this book, which gives us confidence that the *art* component of our research is on very solid ground.

The art component of our research is on very solid ground.

A Note about the Top Five Catalysts for Each Movement

You may have noticed that the order of most influential factors shifts slightly between the four independent categories of spiritual catalysts and the lists of "top five catalysts" for Movements 1 and 2. For example, chart 2-7 (page 42) shows that reflection on Scripture is the most influential personal spiritual practice for each movement. But when we list the top five catalysts for Movements 1 and 2 (charts 3-5 and 3-9, pages 59 and 67), prayer appears to be more influential than reflection on Scripture. The apparent discrepancies are a function of the discriminate analysis.

The top five catalysts for each movement were determined by evaluating all fifty-plus spiritual factors through the discriminate lens, which at times recalibrates the predictability of one factor versus another. That happens when a portion of one factor's predictive power is shared by another. For example, as noted, reflection on Scripture was more highly predictive of spiritual movement than prayer when we looked at personal spiritual practices across the three movements. However, when reflection on Scripture was analyzed alongside all the fifty-plus catalysts, its level of influence was shared to some extent with another factor, possibly the belief in salvation by grace. In this case, because the discriminate analysis is looking for the *best combination* of top five catalysts to explain differences between two segments, it's possible that reflection on Scripture ranked lower than prayer because part of its predictive power is explained by the salvation by grace factor.

Confused? One way to think about this is to consider the food pyramid, which includes five basic food groups: grains, vegetables, fruits, dairy and meat. Each food group could list its most nutritious foods in order. But when you pool all possible foods together looking for the best food plan for a young child, it's likely that not all the top-ranked nutritious foods are on the list. Two reasons account for this. First, when looking for the best combination of nutrients, some foods will be more necessary for a young child than others; that influences the list. Second, some of those foods will have vitamins and nutrients that are redundant with others, so that affects which grains, vegetables and other foods are on the best food plan. So the best combination of foods for a young child won't necessarily include the most nutritious foods in each one of the food group categories, and the rank order of "best" foods could vary as well.

This is analogous to our efforts to find the best combination of spiritual catalysts for the three movements of spiritual growth. The bottom line is that pouring all the spiritual catalysts into one discriminate analysis bucket can shake up the order of the most influential (the top five) because the predictive power of all the factors have to recalibrate in relation to each other.

Research Standards

In summary, we have employed the highest applied research standards available, including a robust qualitative process and three waves of quantitative surveys across hundreds of diverse churches. While there is much more work yet to do, we are confident that the insights and findings in *Follow Me* reflect a very high level of research excellence.

WHO ARE THE 200 CHURCHES IN THE SURVEY?

In August 2007, we offered church leaders attending the WCA Leadership Summit[1] the opportunity for their churches to participate at no cost in the final phase of development of the REVEAL Spiritual Life Survey tool—a survey church leaders could use to assess the spiritual health of their own congregations (for more information, see appendix 4, "What Is the REVEAL Spiritual Life Survey?" on page 156). Approximately 1,700 churches applied for the 500 available spots, including several hundred churches outside the United States. We fielded the survey in two waves: 200 churches in October–November 2007 and the rest in January–February 2008. The findings in *Follow Me* are based on the 200 churches surveyed in October–November 2007.

In selecting the 500 churches, we did our best to strike a balance among various demographic factors, like geographic location, size, denomination and style.[2] While we were limited by the demographics of the 1,700 churches volunteering to participate, we are satisfied that the sample represents a diverse mix of churches, models and formats. What follows provides a brief overview of the 200 churches featured in *Follow Me*.

We did our best to strike a demographic balance among various denominations.

[1] Approximately 107,000 church leaders from thirty-two countries attended the Leadership Summit in 2007. Leaders from the United States and Canada represented 7,200 churches.

[2] We asked all churches who applied for the 500 research spots to select three words out of a dozen options that best described their church. For example: contemporary, conservative, missionary minded, seeker friendly, multicultural, innovative, etc. "Style" refers to the words chosen by church leaders as the best descriptors of their churches.

Geography and Size

Charts A3-1 and A3-2 show the distribution of the 200 churches by geographic location and by size (based on weekend attendance).

Three out of the four geographic regions account for 90 percent of the churches, and each one of those regions accounts for roughly one-third of the sample. The South is more strongly represented due to the influence of the high-population states of Texas and Florida. The Northeast accounts for only 10 percent of the churches.

Weekend attendance shows a fairly balanced distribution across the sample, with 14 percent in the largest two categories (over 2,500) and 16 percent in the smallest categories (under 250). We

Chart A3-1

Geographic Location of the 200 Churches

Geographic Region of US	Geographic Section	Percentage of the 200 Churches Surveyed
Northeast	New England	3%
	Middle Atlantic	7%
Midwest	East North Central	18%
	West North Central	12%
South	South Atlantic	13%
	East South Central	3%
	East South Central	17%
West	Mountain	10%
	Pacific	17%

Chart A3-2
Weekend Attendance of the 200 Churches

Weekend Attendance (adults)	Percentage of the 200 Churches Surveyed
Less than 100	5%
100 – 249	11%
250 – 499	20%
500 – 999	29%
1,000 – 2,499	21%
2,500 – 4,999	10%
5,000 or more	4%

realize this is not necessarily representative of the national distribution of all churches, since a much higher percentage of all churches falls in the under-250 range. But for the purposes of this research phase, we were less concerned about being representative and more concerned about being able to test the viability of fielding the survey across congregations of various sizes.

Denominations and Styles

The mix of denominations and styles was influenced by the types of churches most likely to attend Willow Creek's Leadership Summit (charts A3-3 and A3-4, pages 154–55).

Nondenominational and Baptist churches account for over 50 percent of the 200 churches, though we did achieve a solid mix of other denominations, like Methodist and Lutheran. The style descriptions reflect the three words chosen by each participating church as those that best describe their church. Contemporary, evangelical and seeker friendly lead the way as the most popular choices, though it is important to point out that a large percentage of churches *did not* describe themselves as contemporary, evangelical or seeker friendly. One of our goals was to create a mix of church demographics that wouldn't allow one church model, size or geography to dominate the findings. As a point of interest, Willow Creek Community Church was not included in this phase of our research.

Chart A3-3

Denominations Represented in the 200 Churches

Church Denominations	Percentage of the 200 Churches Surveyed
Nondenominational	32%
Baptist	21%
Methodist	9%
Presbyterian / Reformed	8%
Assembly of God / Church of God / Pentecostal	5%
Evangelical Free	5%
Lutheran	4%
Other	16%

In summary, the demographic mix of the 200 churches included in the findings reported in *Follow Me* provided us with a great opportunity to test the ability of our survey tool to deliver valid and valuable insights to many different kinds of churches. This was our primary

Chart A3-4

Styles Represented in the 200 Churches

Church Style*	Percentage of the 200 Churches Surveyed
Contemporary	70%
Evangelical	61%
Sensitive to Seekers (Seeker Friendly)	61%
Innovative	45%
Visionary	41%
Missionary Minded	38%
Conservative	18%
Multicultural	16%

* Multiple responses were possible. Each church chose up to three descriptors.

goal—to make sure we would be able to deliver as much value to a small, inner-city church as to a large suburban nondenominational church. Our secondary goal was to test the validity of the findings from our earlier research (with approximately thirty churches) against this larger, more diverse database and also to search it for new insights. *Follow Me* describes the new insights, focused primarily on discoveries about the spiritual catalysts most influential to movement along the spiritual continuum. Regarding our primary goal, we're currently in the process of delivering individual reports to the 500 churches about their own survey findings. Based on their feedback, we'll know whether or not that most important goal for this database was accomplished.

appendix **4**

WHAT IS THE REVEAL SPIRITUAL LIFE SURVEY?

The Spiritual Life Survey is a proven way to benchmark and track spiritual growth in a congregation. It moves beyond measures like attendance and financial giving to determine if a church is really making a difference in helping people become more like Christ. This anonymous, congregational online survey is easy to understand, simple to administer and repeatable over time to monitor change. Its large database (more than 157,000 congregants from over 500 churches, twenty denominations and nineteen countries) lets you compare your results with other churches.

Should My Church Use This Tool?

When it comes to spiritual growth, we need to be able to measure the unseen. Churches who use the Spiritual Life Survey receive an in-depth understanding of their congregants' spiritual attitudes, motivations, behaviors and satisfaction. The survey enables church leaders to track over time the movement of their congregation toward Christ, to see if ministry efforts and resource allocations are really contributing to the spiritual health of people in the church.

What Does the Spiritual Life Survey Provide?

- **Three surveys over five years:** A baseline survey and two follow-up surveys. Follow-up surveys can be executed at any time within the five-year window.
- **A Spiritual Life diagnostic report,** benchmarking your church's spiritual profile against the results of any prior surveys as well as other churches in the REVEAL database.
- **Marketing collateral** to help promote the Spiritual Life Survey to your congregation, including sample text for print and e-mail communication and other tools to increase awareness and participation.

What Pastors Are Saying about the
(REVEAL) Spiritual Life Survey

IN MAY 2007, we surveyed over thirty congregations across the United States. Each church received a report detailing what we learned about their congregation. Here is what the pastors of a few of those churches are saying about how the survey results have impacted their ministry.

"We have literally reinvented Discovery Church because of our involvement in this project. I told our leadership it was apparent that we could either use the survey findings to improve what we were already doing, or else we could do a major reinvention of our ministry. We decided to take the reinvention route.

"We began by changing our mission statement. Our previous mission statement had served us well, but in light of the REVEAL findings, we thought it needed to better communicate what people could expect from us as a church (our responsibility) and what the biblical challenge is to every believer (their responsibility). Our new mission statement is: 'Strengthening your pursuit of a Christ-Centered life.' We are evaluating every single ministry, ministry activity, staff position and personnel in light of our new mission statement and strategy. We have a level of clarity, direction, effectiveness and energy that is unlike anything we have experienced in years."

David Loveless, senior pastor
Discovery Church, Orlando, Florida

"Prior to REVEAL, we believed our ministry practices were congruent with the primary findings of the research. After having our congregation surveyed, we see new ways to hone and sharpen both our vision and mission. We now know even more about what facilitates

movement in people's hearts based on their unique place on the spiritual journey. We want to strengthen and support people at each stage and prepare them for ever-increasing responsibility in their own abundant life in Christ."

Bob Bouwer, senior pastor
Faith Church, Dyer, Indiana

"It is extremely difficult as a leader to find 'truth' in an organization. Perhaps even more so in a church where staff and volunteer leaders may fear appearing less than 'kingdom-effective' or spiritual. Or, like most of us, we simply have blind spots in our leadership and ministries.

"Our survey results uncovered fissures in our church's spiritual development and maturity. It was a hard 'truth pill' to swallow, but there were also bright spots. For years we have suspected that serving the underresourced was a critical growth component, especially for mature believers, and have resourced it heavily. It was good to see that validated in the data.

"Each year our leadership team determines strategic initiatives and then the ministry directors develop their own objectives and plans based on those initiatives. We typically establish initiatives based on perceived needs and spiritual intuition. But identifying the needs has been difficult, until now. The REVEAL survey results gave us critical 'truth data.' We also used it to help us determine the topics we need to teach on in order to address the spiritual gaps the survey identified.

"Take the REVEAL survey and discover the truth about your church. And fasten your seatbelt."

Dave Workman, senior pastor
Vineyard Community Church,
Cincinnati, Ohio

ABOUT
THE AUTHORS

Greg L. Hawkins

Greg L. Hawkins is executive pastor of Willow Creek Community Church. Since 1996, he has assisted Senior Pastor Bill Hybels in providing strategic leadership to Willow Creek's five campuses and to the Willow Creek Association. He also serves as point leader for REVEAL, a new initiative within the WCA that utilizes research tools and discoveries to help churches better understand spiritual growth in their congregations. Prior to joining the staff of Willow Creek in 1991, Greg spent five years as a consultant for McKinsey & Company. He has an undergraduate degree in civil engineering from Texas A&M University and an MBA from Stanford University. Greg and his wife, Lynn, live in the Chicago suburbs with their three children.

Cally Parkinson

Cally Parkinson is brand manager for REVEAL, a new initiative within the WCA that utilizes research tools and discoveries to help churches better understand spiritual growth in their congregations. She previously served as the director of communication services at Willow Creek Community Church, a role she took on following a twenty-five-year career at Allstate Insurance Company. At Allstate, Cally held a number of different director- and officer-level positions in strategic planning, research, finance and communications. She has a BA in languages from Depauw University and a master's degree from the American Graduate School of International Management. Cally and her husband, Rich, live in the Chicago suburbs and have two grown children.

VISION, TRAINING, RESOURCES
FOR PREVAILING CHURCHES

This resource was created to serve you and to help you build a local church that prevails. It is just one of many ministry tools published by the Willow Creek Association.

The Willow Creek Association (WCA) was created in 1992 to serve a rapidly growing number of churches from across the denominational spectrum that are committed to helping unchurched people become fully devoted followers of Christ. Membership in the WCA now numbers over 12,000 Member Churches worldwide from more than ninety denominations.

The Willow Creek Association links like-minded Christian leaders with each other and with strategic vision, training and resources in order to help them build prevailing churches designed to reach their redemptive potential. Here are some of the ways the WCA does that.

- **The Leadership Summit**—A once-a-year, two-day conference to envision and equip Christians with leadership gifts and responsibilities. Presented live on Willow Creek's campus as well as via satellite broadcast to over 135 locations across North America—plus more than eighty international cities via videocast—this event is designed to increase the leadership effectiveness of pastors, ministry staff, volunteer church leaders and Christians in the marketplace.

- **Ministry-Specific Conferences**—Throughout the year the WCA hosts a variety of conferences and training events—both at Willow Creek's main campus and offsite, across North America and around the world. These events are for church leaders and volunteers in areas such as small groups, children's ministry, student ministry, preaching and teaching, the arts and stewardship.

- **Willow Creek Resources ®**—Provides churches with trusted and field-tested ministry resources in such areas as leadership, volunteer ministries, spiritual formation, stewardship, evangelism, small groups, children's ministry, student ministry, the arts and more.

- **WCA Member Benefits**—Includes substantial discounts to WCA training events, a 20 percent discount on all Willow Creek Resources®, *Defining Moments* monthly audio journal for leaders, quarterly *Willow* magazine, access to a Members-Only section on WillowNet, monthly communications and more. Member Churches also receive special discounts and premier services through the WCA's growing number of ministry partners—Select Service Providers—and save an average of $500 annually depending on the level of engagement.

For specific information about WCA conferences, resources, membership and other ministry services contact:

WILLOW

Willow Creek Association
P.O. Box 3188 • Barrington, IL 60011-3188 • Phone: 847-570-9812 • Fax: 847-765-5046
www.willowcreek.com